California HOME

© 2013 by TGS International, a wholly owned subsidiary of
Christian Aid Ministries, Berlin, Ohio.

All rights reserved. No part of this book may be used, reproduced, or stored in any retrieval system, in any form or by any means, electronic or mechanical, without written permission from the publisher except for brief quotations embodied in critical articles and reviews.

ISBN 978-1-939084-25-5
Cover design: Megan Yoder
Text layout design: Megan Yoder
Printed in the USA
For more information about Christian Aid Ministries, see page 174.

A true story of one family's life in the West. Names are fictitious.

Published by:
TGS International
P.O. Box 355
Berlin, Ohio 44610 USA
Phone: 330·893·4828
Fax: 330·893·2305
www.tgsinternational.com

TGS000647

California HOME

Fonda Good

chapter one

VANDERBILT GAVE A WARNING GROWL AS a late-model gray car bounced over the bumpy road up the mountain. At a big blue house perched on the mountainside, the whole Brenneman family waited on the front deck.

Olive watched the driver hesitate before the car roared up the last stretch to her home. She was as excited as the rest to see great-uncle Ephraim and great-aunt Bonnie, but she was twelve now—too old to jump up and down like her younger brothers and sisters.

Dad looked over the railing and stroked his beard as Uncle Ephraim parked along the steep lane. "I wouldn't have thought Uncle Ephraim was rich enough for that kind of car. But . . . of course, it's a rental car. What am I thinking? They drove here from the airport in Los Angeles."

"It's a beau-u-u-tiful car!" said thirteen-year-old Leonard.

"I'm sure I wouldn't know it from the next one down the

street," Olive laughed. "But I don't care what kind of car Uncle Ephraim drives. I like his hat."

Uncle Ephraim and Aunt Bonnie slowly crawled out of the fancy car and walked toward the house. Dad and Mom walked out to meet them, but the children stood still. A few moments before, they had been jumping and talking, but suddenly they were subdued and shy. They hung back, waiting for the adults.

Then Olive changed her mind. A twelve-year-old was big enough to introduce herself. Leonard followed her, and the rest of the children inched along behind.

Uncle Ephraim and Aunt Bonnie smiled and shook hands with everyone, in the formal way uncles and aunts do.

"Now you must introduce them all, Michelle," Aunt Bonnie said to Mom. "I remember only Leonard and Olive, since they were born in Ohio."

"Well, line up by age, children," Mom told them. Giggling nervously, the children complied.

"Oh, no," Madeline whispered. "Now she'll notice I'm shorter than Andrea."

Mom started down the line. "After Olive comes Madeline. Then there's Andrea, Tabitha, Sandra, Florence, and baby Zachary."

"I see," said Aunt Bonnie. Then she pointed at Andrea. "I thought you were next to Olive."

"Everybody thinks that," ten-year-old Madeline said. "Andrea's only nine, but she's bigger, that's why. I have to get her hand-me-downs even if I'm older."

Aunt Bonnie laughed. "That's exactly how it was with my sister and me when we were young. But when you get old, you are just glad to be healthy, and you don't care much about being a few inches shorter."

Olive watched Uncle Ephraim. She could tell just by watching him that he was an interesting person. Before he came, Dad had called him a colorful character, and Olive knew what that meant. He wouldn't be just any old guest. Uncle Ephraim would be a person to remember.

Uncle Ephraim looked out over the valley, shaking his head. "What a view!" he exclaimed. "And to think we were in Ohio this morning. How do you stay on this mountainside and keep from sliding off, Alan?" he asked, looking at Dad.

"Very carefully," Dad replied, and everyone laughed as they walked up the steps to the house.

Sandra took Aunt Bonnie's hand. "We're going to have a wiener roast," she announced with an important air. "Do you like wieners?"

"Of course I do," Aunt Bonnie said. "Do you?"

In just a few minutes, the Brenneman girls forgot their shyness and chattered with Aunt Bonnie like old friends. Mom gathered the things for the wiener roast, and they all headed out to the back yard.

"A grill?" asked Uncle Ephraim with surprise. "I expected to see a bonfire."

"Oh, no," Dad shook his head. "It's fire season. We can't burn anything but charcoal right now. If we started a fire on this mountainside, I'd be broke for the rest of my life. The person who starts the fire must pay to fight it, you know."

"If we make too much smoke, that's a problem too," Olive added. "Once, we grilled a whole bunch of chicken, and the firemen came."

Uncle Ephraim looked at her curiously. "Did they really?"

Dad finished the story. "It's true; they did. We had put the chicken on before the coals had died down enough, and it did make a lot of smoke. Someone from the highway reported a fire, and so they came to check it out. We often wished we would have gotten a picture of those firemen all dressed in full gear, peering down at our chicken on the grill."

"Interesting," Uncle Ephraim said. He stood for a few minutes taking in the scenery around him. "Do you know the one word I would use to sum up your land here?" he asked, looking at Leonard and Olive. "The word is 'dry.' "

Olive looked down at the sandy soil under her feet. Nothing much grew in the back yard, even in the spring when it was wet. What would it be like to live in a land where plants were green and growing in your back yard?

Seven-year-old Tabitha was still chattering to Aunt Bonnie. "We have lizards," she announced.

Aunt Bonnie shivered. "I don't like lizards very well."

"Why?" Tabitha asked in surprise. "They're so much fun to catch, Aunt Bonnie."

"I suppose they are," Aunt Bonnie agreed. "But don't catch one for me. I saw one in Florida one time, and that's all I care to see."

The girls looked at each other. Aunt Bonnie was really in the dark on lizards. Why would a person hate them?

After prayer everyone took turns roasting hot dogs over the grill. Olive looked at the wiener roast with new eyes. It *was* rather strange to roast hot dogs on a grill, now that she thought of it. It seemed kind of like cheating. What fun it would be to have a big roaring fire!

"I thought you could grow oranges in California," said Uncle Ephraim. "I don't see any orange trees."

"We can't grow them right here," Olive spoke up. "We're up too high."

Uncle Ephraim gazed out over the valley before he spoke. "I see. Well, what is the elevation here?"

Olive looked at Leonard. He was the one for the technical details.

"Right here it's about five thousand feet above sea level," he began. "But we're right on the edge of a mountain range that drops you down into the San Joaquin Valley, and that's around five hundred feet above sea level. If you go down into the valley, you can see plenty of orange trees."

"You're quite the knowledgeable young man," Uncle Ephraim said, looking at Leonard in his intense way.

Leonard shrugged. "It's just stuff I hear Dad say."

Uncle Ephraim kept right on looking at Leonard. Finally he spoke. "You are just the spitting image of your dad too," he said, breaking into a sideways smile.

Leonard and Olive smiled too. There was something about Uncle Ephraim that made you want to smile inside the whole time you were with him. Maybe it was his squat, short-brimmed hat that he always wore when he was outside the house, with his wide round eyes underneath taking everything in.

Mom tried to get Aunt Bonnie to sit down while the girls did the dishes, but she would have none of it. "I sat all day," she protested. So Aunt Bonnie washed the dishes while Olive and Madeline dried.

"Do you have a garden?" Aunt Bonnie asked them.

Olive shook her head. "No, Dad says the soil is bad, and the animals will eat everything right up. Besides, you have to water everything, and it's not worth it if the food goes to the animals anyway."

Aunt Bonnie clucked in sympathy. "My, I don't know what I'd do if I couldn't have a garden. We have a big produce patch. The grandchildren help, and we split the profits with them."

"That would be fun!" exclaimed Madeline. "I wish I were your grandchild!"

Olive nodded in agreement. "Don't you have to water at all?"

"Oh my, no. We let the Lord rain it down. Some years it could use some watering, but other years it's too wet."

Olive couldn't imagine that much rain. Here on the mountain where they lived it usually didn't rain all summer long, and if it did, it was just a little.

Andrea walked up just as the dishes were done. "Aunt Bonnie, is it true that Uncle Ephraim can walk on his hands?"

"Now who told you that?" Aunt Bonnie wanted to know.

"Grandpa told us he could," Andrea explained.

Uncle Ephraim had overheard from the living room. "Do you want me to show you whether or not your grandpa was right?" he asked.

"Yes," the children chorused, and Uncle Ephraim carefully bent over. Olive held her breath. What if he fell? But Uncle Ephraim knew what he was doing. Ever so carefully, he lifted his black shoes in the air, and soon he was standing on his head. Then away he walked. The Brenneman children laughed and laughed. They wondered how many other tricks Uncle Ephraim could do.

Uncle Ephraim was breathing hard when he righted himself. "Next time I visit you I might be too old for that," he said, and Aunt Bonnie was muttering that there probably wouldn't be a next time.

"We missed your family at the Brenneman gathering," Uncle Ephraim said when he had caught his breath.

"We missed you too," Mom said. "I always wish we weren't so far away when there are family gatherings. I sure would like to see your family and all the rest."

"What did the children do at the family gathering?" Olive asked.

"Oh, Uncle Clarence rented a little train made out of metal drums, and they pulled it with a tractor. Did the children have fun in that! I think it was running almost all day," said Aunt Bonnie.

The children listened with open mouths. What fun!

Leonard was busy figuring out how the train had been made, but Olive's thoughts were elsewhere. She hadn't realized the many things they missed by living on the West Coast. The more she thought about it, the more unfair it seemed. The people in Ohio had it nice. They could enjoy big, green back yards and huge bonfires. They had huge gardens watered by God. In Ohio, there were big family gatherings with free train rides. On the other hand, in California, they thought it was special to do something as normal as roasting hotdogs over the grill. It didn't seem fair.

"I think we'd better head to bed," Dad suggested after they had visited a while longer. "Uncle Ephraim and Aunt Bonnie are still used to Eastern time."

"Yes," agreed Uncle Ephraim. "It has been a long day. Three hours longer than normal, in fact. But tomorrow I want to see that valley with the orange trees."

"Olive, take this bucket of water out to smother the last of the coals," said Mom. "You know Dad can't sleep if there's a fire burning."

After Olive put out the fire, she stood on the deck and looked up at the stars and the moon. But she wasn't *really* looking at the stars and the moon. She was still thinking. *Maybe when I grow up I'll move back to Ohio. It seems things are so much better there. Maybe Grandma or Grandpa will need someone to take care of them.* Olive felt a little guilty hoping Grandma and Grandpa would need care someday. She really hoped they would be healthy until the day they died. *Well, I could teach school or something.* Olive looked around her with distaste. She couldn't see much in the dark, but she knew what was there. There were the juniper trees and sagebrush, the wild elderberry trees and the fire ants with their painful stings. The diamondback rattlesnakes and the coyotes were lurking somewhere too. California didn't seem friendly to Olive. Not at all.

chapter two

"GET IT!" MADELINE YELLED TO LEONARD. Leonard lunged frantically and came up grinning with a lizard in his hand. Olive looked up from the corner of the sandbox where she had been blocking the lizard's exit. You had to be on your toes to catch lizards, but Leonard was pretty good at it.

Mom had walked out to hang out the diapers, so the children showed their new friend to her. Mom only made a face.

"I must say I don't care much for lizards. I grew up in Ohio like Aunt Bonnie, you know," she said, looking sideways at the lizard. "It's a good thing Aunt Bonnie isn't here anymore, or I'm afraid you'd have her screaming. We didn't have lizards back in our growing up days."

"That *is* sad," Madeline said sympathetically.

"Don't worry—we didn't feel like we were missing

anything, and I still don't," Mom added.

"Well, I'm going to give this lizard to Vanderbilt," Leonard said, dashing off. Olive was shocked and furious. Feeding a lizard to a dog was mean. Leonard was gone, so it was too late to try to talk sense into him.

"Mom," Olive complained, "I can't believe you didn't stop him. I mean, that lizard is one of God's creatures too. He can't help he is a lizard. That Leonard doesn't even have a heart!"

Mom was busy hanging up the diapers, and she only said, "I'm sure that lizard will never even know what happened to him. You must remember that animals don't have emotions like humans."

"I know, but . . ." Just then Leonard returned, and Olive looked at him with disgust.

"He loved it!" Leonard laughed. "He ate it in one gulp."

"I can't believe you would do such a thing." Olive was still upset. "How would you like if a great big giant came and caught you and fed you to the . . . the . . . lions?"

"C'mon, Olive." Leonard took on a mature air. "Don't you remember what we learned in science class? About the food chain? God made it that way—you know, the bugs eat the grass, the lizards eat the bugs, and the dogs eat the lizards . . ."

"I smell smoke," Tabitha commented from where she was swinging.

The lizard discussion was forgotten as the Brenneman children sniffed the air. Sure enough, they all smelled smoke.

There was something exciting about the smell of smoke. It went along with summertime and brave firemen and helicopters.

"I see the smoke," Olive yelled as her eyes scanned the horizon. "It looks like it's not too far away."

They all saw it now. Mom had joined them, and they all watched as the mushroom of smoke billowed higher and higher right in front of their eyes.

"I'm so glad there's a fire." Andrea's eyes were shining. Immediately the rest of the children turned to look at her.

"You shouldn't be glad there's a fire. What if someone gets hurt? What if it burns someone up?" Olive reprimanded.

Andrea looked thoughtful. "I guess maybe I shouldn't be glad there's a fire, but maybe we can see planes."

"I know." Olive decided to be honest. "I think it's exciting too. But a fire can hurt people and costs a lot of money, so we have to think of that."

The phone began ringing. Mom ran to answer it, and the children quietly watched the smoke. It was filling the whole canyon now, and they could hardly see the town right below them.

"That was Dad," Mom said when she returned. "He said the fire is right over by the shop, and it is heading straight for Uncle Craig's place. It hardly looks like they'll be able to save the house."

The children stood stock still and looked at Mom. Surely that couldn't be. What if their cousins and Aunt Judy couldn't get out of the house in time?

Olive looked at the smoke again. Why had she thought it seemed exciting? Now it looked sinister, like a monster that was eating up everything in its path. Olive heard a sniffle behind her. Andrea was crying. "I didn't mean it when I said I'm glad there's a fire," she sobbed. "What if Uncle Craig's house gets burned up?"

Mom put her arm around Andrea. "Don't worry, children," she said. "God knows where the fire is, and He will do what's best for Uncle Craig's family. I'm quite sure they're out of the house. But why don't we pray for them?"

The children knelt with Mom in a circle on the ground and took turns praying for Uncle Craig's family. Olive was praying silently, even when it wasn't her turn. "Please, dear God, let Uncle Craig's family be safe," she prayed over and over. Mom prayed last. There was something comforting about hearing Mom speak so matter-of-factly to God about the situation. They all felt better when they got up from their knees.

"There comes a helicopter," shouted Leonard, and at the same time they heard the phone ring. Mom rushed into the house again, and the children followed to see who had called. Mom was soon off the phone. She looked vastly relieved. "Dad said the fire is past Uncle Craig's house now, and the firemen saved the house. He wondered if Aunt Judy and the children can come here."

The children immediately forgot their fear as they cheered and ran back outside to see the helicopter flying overhead. It was a firefighting helicopter, and the white collapsible bucket that hung underneath it looked like a giant bag filled with water.

Olive stayed inside with Mom. "Do we have electricity?" she asked. Things seemed just a little extra quiet. Mom tried the lights, and sure enough, the electricity was off.

Mom shivered. "This is getting too close to home. I hope Dad comes home from work soon."

"Hey, look!" yelled Leonard through the screen door. "See that plane dropping out of the clouds?" Olive ran to the porch and watched as the plane headed into the smoke to dump its load of red fire retardant. Olive wished they could see it being dumped. She remembered the time they had been in the village of Lebec and had stayed behind watching the planes, even after the rest of the village had evacuated. It had been exciting to see the streaks of red behind the planes. She had pretended that she was in a war-torn country, and the planes were dropping bombs. She hadn't pretended long, though, because it wasn't a nice thought.

Almost every summer in California brought new experiences with wildfires. "Remember the time when Dad almost got colored red?" Leonard asked. Olive sure did remember! That summer day Dad and some of his co-workers from the construction crew had tried to save a brand new house on top of a little mountain. The men hadn't wanted to see their hard work go up in smoke, and since no one was living there yet, they had been afraid the firemen wouldn't pay much attention to it. Dad had been in a skid loader when he saw a fire-fighting plane flying over him. He had backed up his skid loader just in time to avoid getting hit with the red powder.

"Here's Aunt Judy," Madeline announced, and they all crowded around her to hear about the excitement.

"We had gotten out of the house a while ago," Aunt Judy told Mom. "The policemen had driven by with their loudspeakers, telling us to get out, like they always do. We were sitting by the road, and Craig parked the car with some of the children in it by the shed, ready to go. He had just dashed back into the house to get some photo albums that we had forgotten to grab. When he came out, it was so smoky he could hardly see, and a fireman told him in no uncertain terms to leave.

"It's mainly a grass fire," Aunt Judy continued, "and since there's not much grass around here, I think they'll have it out soon. But our house will be smoky. You know Conrad has asthma, and I wonder if we should take him back tonight."

"Come in," said Mom, "you know you can stay here as long as you need to. Besides, it's getting chilly out here. That's the desert air for you. Warm as long as the sun is up and chilly as soon as it goes down."

Olive went inside and listened to the ladies talk. Uncle Craig's children didn't seem in the mood to play. They were a little dazed, in fact. Olive figured she would be too if everything was normal and then, all of a sudden, everyone was running out the lane and watching a fire go right past the house.

"I wonder if our pig is all burnt up," said Cousin Lisa sadly, and the Brenneman cousins looked at each other in alarm.

"Hmm," Adam said. "I guess maybe we'll find a little bacon and ham left to pick at when we get home."

That's just what Leonard would have said, Olive thought. *Boys think of the most awful things.*

The house got darker and darker. "I wonder when we'll get electricity," Mom said. "And what can we have for supper? We have no way to heat it up, whatever it is."

"Yes, we do," Leonard piped up. "The stove uses gas—it's just the pilot light that won't work."

"Ahh, you're right," Mom agreed, smiling at Leonard. "I'm glad we have a man around here."

Soon the women were busy cooking spaghetti. Olive looked around in the semi-darkness, trying to find some candles, but she couldn't find any. Mom had just housecleaned, and when Mom housecleaned, well, look out. If anything hadn't been used recently, Mom just sent it to Goodwill Industries for them to sell at their thrift store.

The two families were ready to eat when the men came home. Doug Remington was with them.

"Welcome, Doug," said Mom through the darkness. "Is your house smoky too?"

"It might be a little," Doug said in his nervous way. "But I was over helping Craig open the windows in his house, and the men kindly invited me to stop by for a solid meal."

Mom laughed. "They must have faith. It's good we have a

gas stove or we'd have to eat crackers and cheerios."

"That would have been fine. That would have been fine," smiled Doug. "I'm not used to eating fancy."

I know he's not, Olive thought to herself. Doug had once been homeless, and he looked like he could be still. He was thin to the point of being gaunt, and he had a long, untrimmed beard. He had first come to the community looking for work. Marlin Hines, a man from their church who had a lawn care business, had given Doug a job. After a few months, however, Doug had run away, stealing Marlin's minivan. But a year later he was back. He said his conscience made him return. He brought the van back and worked hard to make up for running away.

Doug was a kind and thoughtful man, but he still hadn't given his life to God. And he was always nervous. He had taken too many drugs and drunk too much alcohol, and they had affected his body and mind. "The wages of sin are hard," Dad had told the children. "Doug will never be a healthy man, unless God heals his broken body. We must show him Christian love, and maybe he will give his life to God."

"Okay, children," said Dad, breaking into Olive's thoughts, "don't we have any flashlights around here? Here, let me get my big one out in the truck."

It was cozy to eat by the light of the flashlight, and Uncle Craig told a story that made them all laugh. "I talked to one of the firemen," he said. "This fireman stayed behind to make sure our house was all right after the fire went through. He told me what happened to our pig. Another fireman noticed that the pig was awfully close to the fire and smoke, so he turned on the water hose by the house and gave it a drink, and then he just kept spraying water on the pig until the fire had passed."

"I guess this helps us not to complain about paying taxes," Dad said. "California has a pretty organized fire department and men who are willing to risk their lives."

Olive could hardly believe the pig story. The discussion made her think more about firemen. What would it be like to live in a place where the people didn't know how to fight fires? To live in southern California without a really good fire department would be pretty hard. The summer before, there had been a really big fire that had burned thousands of acres. It had burned for a month straight, and a few houses even burned. Olive remembered feeling little pieces of ash floating down on her arms when the fire was sixty miles away. But firemen had worked night and day to keep it under control, and finally they had put out the fire. Without them, a lot of people would lose their houses every year. Why, the firemen even cared about saving a pig!

Everyone gathered around in the dark living room for family worship. Dad read the Bible, and they all sang together. They had to sing from memory because the rays of the flashlight didn't reach very far.

Uncle Craig wanted to sing "Someone to Thank." As they sang, "There is Someone who daily my needs doth supply, / These good things don't just happen, there's Someone on high," Olive was deep in thought. Dad and Mom had always told her that God was in control of her life, and she believed it. But lately she had been noticing things for herself. Things like fires. Would God have let Uncle Craig's house burn if they had not prayed? It made Olive feel good inside to think that God had answered their prayers. Then she thought of all the other people whose houses were in the same path as Uncle Craig's. Maybe they didn't know who to turn to when they were in trouble. If they hadn't prayed, they'd better be glad that there were Christians who prayed for them.

Olive looked at Doug, fidgeting in his chair. She wondered if he, too, was thinking.

"You know," Uncle Craig commented, "if we had stayed back East, we wouldn't have to worry about big wildfires."

Olive looked at Uncle Craig closely. Did he wish they had? Was he feeling the same way she had the other evening when Uncle Ephraim was visiting?

Dad smiled at Uncle Craig. "You can go back there and be hit by a tornado, if you want."

Uncle Craig chuckled. "I didn't finish my thought. I wasn't saying I wish I hadn't moved out here. I was just thinking about it—how we sometimes forget how much our lives are in God's hands wherever we are. There are dangers in California and Ohio, and the same God decides when our time is up."

"That's right, Craig. That's right," Doug said. Olive hoped he meant it. Maybe he was starting to see the truth about God.

There are fewer dangers in Ohio, though, Olive thought to herself. *They don't have to worry about earthquakes, big wildfires, or rattlesnakes.*

"I wonder if the fire is out," Leonard said, breaking the silence.

"It is," Dad's voice boomed through the darkness. "I called preacher Abram a little while ago, and he said most of the firemen are gone. Of course, a few will stay around all night to watch the hot spots that are still smoking. And to take care of the pigs," he added with a laugh.

Olive walked over to Leonard and whispered, "That fireman cared more about animals than you did this afternoon."

"Maybe he fed the pig a lizard for his supper," Leonard shot back, just as quietly.

chapter three

OLIVE SETTLED BACK ON THE HARD SEAT of the old white church bus and hugged her knees. She was tired of working and glad this day had finally come. As she looked around at her brothers and sisters, with their hair neatly combed and their next-to-best clothes on, all the work they'd had to do in preparation for this special day faded into the background.

It was Aunt Marge's thirtieth birthday, and they were going to the ocean. Even though Aunt Marge wasn't really their aunt, the Brennemans wanted to celebrate her birthday just like family, since she was such a special person and her real family lived way back East. After all, Aunt Marge had come the whole way from Ohio to help Mom and Dad raise their family. She was a cousin to Mom, so they were family, in a way, and Olive liked the saying, "blood runs thick." She wasn't sure what it meant really, only she knew it meant family is special, even if they aren't perfect. Uncle Jim was going with them today too, because Aunt Marge was his cousin, and they were friends. Uncle Jim was a bachelor—the fun, comfortable kind.

Olive looked out the window. It was a beautiful day to be alive, and she was excited about going to the ocean. Trips to the ocean were one good thing about living in southern California.

The seats in the bus were high, so Olive couldn't see the adults, but she could hear them talking.

"I still can't believe this," Aunt Marge was saying. "I should have noticed that Michelle was more organized than usual to tell me a few months ago that they had something planned on my birthday. I never imagined it would be all *this!*"

Olive heard Mom laugh.

"Really," said Uncle Jim, "we told you ahead of time because we didn't want you to think no one cared that you were turning thirty. We didn't want you to feel sad the whole week before your birthday."

"Oh, stop," Aunt Marge protested. "Do you think my birthday is that big a deal? I had almost forgotten what day it was."

"I'm still enough of a child to look forward to my birthday," Uncle Jim told her, "and you're only two years older than I am."

"Ooooh, beautiful," said Madeline from the seat beside Olive, and Olive turned to look out the window. The green hills were aflame with wild flowers. Olive drank in the beauty of those hills. The hills close to their hometown of Frazier Park grew some wild flowers every year, but never in such quantities as she had just seen.

"Where do the wildflowers come from, Olive?" Tabitha asked from the seat beside her. Olive looked down at Tabitha, who was sitting primly in the bus seat with her hands folded in her lap. Her collar was lying flat, and her shoes were tied with bows that were just the same size on each shoe.

"Where do they?" Tabitha persisted.

"Oh, I forgot you asked," Olive said. "Do you think I'm a science book?"

"No, Olive, but you know a lot of things." Tabitha looked up at her trustingly, and Olive felt the weight of her six years of school.

"It had to be God who planted them because I don't think anyone knows when they first started growing there. But every year that we get enough rain, there they are. Only if we get too much rain, the grass chokes them out, and it's the same as if we didn't get enough."

"Did you know that the poppy is the California state flower?" asked a voice from the back. It was Leonard. Olive had decided long ago that Leonard should be a schoolteacher when he grew up. He liked social studies and science as much as Olive struggled with them! Olive liked to study health, but she hated trying to remember facts about the states and the different kinds of rocks and flowers.

"Most of the flowers by our house are poppies," Madeline said, and Olive nodded.

"They're mostly poppies with some purple lupines. But the ones that we just saw must have had other kinds mixed in too, because they were prettier than the ones at home!"

"Do you think it's true that if you go to sleep in a bed of poppies, you'll never wake up?" Tabitha asked.

Olive shook her head. "I don't think it's true. People say that because a drug called opium comes from a certain kind of poppies. Opium puts people to sleep, but I don't think you'd get enough from a few crushed poppies."

"Now we know what to do when hard times come and we have to get a tooth pulled," Leonard said. "Hey, I wonder if too many poppy breezes floated through the window for Andrea," he added. The Brenneman children all turned to look at Andrea. Sure enough, she was curled up in the seat—fast asleep.

"How can she sleep on such an exciting day?" Olive wondered. Madeline just shook her head.

Five-year-old Sandra walked down the aisle of the bus. She thought it was wonderful to be allowed out of a car seat for the whole trip. She was pretending to be a flight attendant, and she looked at each passenger carefully to make sure all seat belts were buckled before take-off. Then she came to Andrea.

"She looks just like Muffy," Sandra said, and the rest of the children had to agree. She *did* remind them of the way their cat curled up on their beds when she sneaked into the house.

"That's good if she sleeps," said Leonard. "Now she'll be sweet for the rest of the day. Why don't you sleep too?" he said to Olive.

Olive made a face at him. She knew he was trying to ruffle her fur, but in light of the special day, she decided to say nothing. He could sit back there and laugh at his own jokes.

Olive listened to the hum of the bus wheels, and she thought more about Aunt Marge's birthday celebration. Mom had invited a few special guests for breakfast, and she wanted the house spotless—without Aunt Marge's help. Olive thought some of it was totally unnecessary. What did order in the toy closet have to do with a special breakfast for Aunt Marge? Olive made up her mind that if she ever had a family, she wouldn't mind if things weren't completely in order. Nobody really needed to poke into your dresser drawers unless you died. Then you wouldn't be embarrassed anyway. She would make sure her babies were clean, though, because Olive couldn't stand dirty babies. She liked babies *in their place*, but they had to smell good and not be crying. Maybe she could hire Madeline to help her if she ever had a family. Madeline loved babies—all the more, it seemed, if they *were* dirty or crying.

Olive smiled as she remembered the look on Aunt Marge's face as she had walked into the house to help Mom like she always did on Saturdays, and there they were, all waiting to eat breakfast with her. Mom had made a fancy breakfast with yogurt parfaits in plastic goblets by everybody's plates and other things that the Brenneman family didn't have except on special occasions. Olive had wanted to decorate the table with sagebrush. She loved the smell of sagebrush and thought it would go so well with Mom's off-white candles. But Mom shook her head.

"You know Aunt Marge has allergies," she said, and Olive admitted that it might ruin the weekend for Aunt Marge if she started sneezing. The table was really pretty, even without the sagebrush. Olive soaked it all in eagerly. She loved fine dining, even though Dad and Mom had often told her that life just couldn't be one big party.

It was funny, Olive had to admit. Mom couldn't figure it out, and Olive couldn't either. Why did she abhor girlish things one minute and love beauty the next? Olive couldn't explain it, but sometimes she seemed like two different people. One was the little girl Olive who didn't like to clean the house, and the other was the grown-up Olive who looked around when the house was a mess, and decided that her own house would be perfect someday.

They were getting close to the ocean now. Aunt Marge had never seen the elephant seals before, so their first stop was going to be the San Simeon beach. The bus slowed down, and Dad turned in to the seal-viewing spot. Olive was ready to get out under the clear blue sky after sitting in the bus for three hours. The rest of the children seemed restless too, because when the bus door opened, they all tumbled out at once.

"Stay close," Dad called out. The children slowed down

and waited for the adults to catch up.

As much noise as the Brenneman family made on their way across the parking lot, it was amazing how silent they became when they looked over the railing at the elephant seals. It was awesome to see God's wild creatures right in front of their eyes and know that no one had confined them there. The elephant seals looked like great big slugs lying in uneven rows along the beach. Who told them to swim to San Simeon every year?

A lady standing nearby had a little badge on her shirt that said "Friends of the Elephant Seals." She was a volunteer who was there to tell tourists about the seals and help with safety.

"Where are the males?" Dad asked her. "The last time I was here, the bulls were fighting."

"Out to sea," she explained. "You'll notice that it's mostly the babies that are here right now. The females are heading back out to sea, and the babies are left alone to learn to swim."

"They have to learn?"

The lady nodded. "Most of them learn, but some of them die trying."

Olive shivered. Poor things. They couldn't help that they were born as seals that couldn't swim. She wondered why God made them to be sea creatures without putting in them the directions to swim.

Aunt Marge looked at the seals for a long time. "Are there always seals here when you come?" she asked Olive.

"There are seals here on the Piedras Blancas rookery every month of the year except August," explained the elephant seal lady, who had overheard the question. "It's either the molting females, the fighting and breeding males, or the baby seals."

"How do they get their food?" Aunt Marge wondered.

"They don't," the lady smiled. "For the months they're here, the females fast. When the babies are born, they get fat from nursing, and then when the females leave, the babies lose one-half of their body weight until they learn to swim and get their own food in the water."

"Maybe they learn to swim because they're hungry," Olive suggested to Aunt Marge. "But some of them die. Why do you think God lets some of the babies die?"

Aunt Marge shook her head. "I don't like to think of it. Maybe God knew there would be too many if they didn't."

"Thinking of food makes me hungry," said Leonard, who had been listening studiously to the elephant seal lady.

It *was* lunchtime. Some of the children had fun feeding the sea gulls while the grown-ups set out the picnic. Olive decided she was too big to play with the little children and helped Mom get the food ready. The more the day progressed, the more Olive saw how wise Mom had been to plan so far ahead. It had taken a lot of work to prepare for this event. She started to feel guilty that she hadn't helped more willingly. Mom had often told Olive that she was looking forward to the day when Olive would be mature enough to stop complaining and just pitch in. Olive sighed.

She would try harder.

Mom saw that the children were feeding the gulls potato chips, and she soon put a stop to that. "I didn't buy chips to waste on gulls," she said. "Chips are expensive, and I'd rather spend my money on hungry people than hungry birds."

The salty ocean breezes were pleasant, and the Brenneman family took plenty of time to relax and eat their lunch. After the children were done eating, they ran out on the pier to look down at the waves. As they walked, they watched the fishermen scattered here and there along the pier. Some of them had a few fish in their buckets, and one even had a lobster.

"I thought lobsters had two big pincers," Leonard said, studying the creature in a fisherman's bucket. The grizzled old fisherman gave him a lopsided smile.

"You must be from the East Coast," he said. "The Atlantic lobster has big pincers, but not the Pacific one."

"Thank you," said Leonard politely, and Olive made a mental note to tell Mom and Dad that new piece of information.

After lunch was cleaned up, Mom gave Aunt Marge a friendship quilt that she and the ladies from church had been working on for a whole year. It had been hard for Mom to keep such a major project a secret when it was going on right in front of Aunt Marge's nose. Aunt Marge had a few indications that something was in the air, but she was still surprised to see it. As she looked over all the names, she got tears in her eyes. Olive knew Mom wanted Aunt Marge to feel loved this weekend, and it seemed to Olive that Aunt Marge would feel wrapped in love if she was wrapped in that quilt full of the names of the people who loved her.

"All right, Michelle," Aunt Marge said to Mom. "Are these all the surprises that you have cooked up for the weekend? I'm not sure I can handle much more."

Why did she say that? Olive wondered, looking at Aunt Marge. *I could handle any amount of good surprises like that!*

Mom laughed, "That's the last one, Marge." Aunt Marge gave Mom a hug before they refolded the quilt. Then it was time to get on the bus again. They were planning to spend the rest of the afternoon at Morrow Bay.

It took only a few minutes to get to the bay. "Oh, no," Dad said. "Morrow Bay is loaded with people. Shall we just go to Montaña de Oro State Park?"

"Yes!" the children chorused.

The adults all agreed, and in a short time they were walking Montaña de Oro's beautiful wilderness trail. The trail wound its way right along the ocean. Something about the blue sky and the smell of sagebrush along the trail, combined with the rush of the waves and the endless horizon, made Olive feel small and lonely.

"Children," Dad warned, "watch the cliffs!" Olive trembled to think of one of them falling headlong down over those cliffs and being dashed into pieces at the bottom. She moved a little farther away from the edge. Leonard,

Madeline, and Tabitha stayed a good distance away too, but Andrea kept walking as close as she thought was safe. There was so much to see down there!

They had walked about half a mile along the trail when they found the steps that took them down to the water's edge. One section had tide pools in the rocks that held water after the tide had gone out. These pools contained all kinds of fun things, like starfish, anemones, and little shrimp-like creatures.

Beside the tide pools was the sandy shore. The children were soon absorbed in finding strange sea creatures. Even Zachary was digging in the great big sandbox.

Olive sat on a rock and looked out across the ocean. She thought about Christopher Columbus and the dangerous job of being a sailor in days gone by. How would it be to get on a ship and sail far away across the horizon to where you couldn't see land anymore? Olive thought maybe she would kind of like to be an old-fashioned sailor. Waking up to sea breezes every morning and eating fish for breakfast sounded kind of fun.

Next Olive thought about God. Something about the wide expanse of water made her feel the power of God. The rolling waves seemed to say, "We have so much strength that you'd be like a toothpick in our grasp." It made Olive wonder how people could say that the world started from a big bang. There was no way a bang could have created this vast ocean nor could it have made the little anemones that the children were playing with right now. Olive had always believed in God just because that's what her parents had taught her, but lately she had been thinking more about these things. She wanted to understand more about the way God worked.

The children could have played for hours and hours, but far too soon Dad said it was time to go. As they slowly walked back to the trail, something caught Olive's eye. It was someone's sandal, a man's sturdy sandal, and Olive picked it up. "Hey, Dad," she called, "can we take this home?"

"Whatever for?" he asked.

"To send to another country," she said, walking over to Dad.

"No," Dad replied. "There's only one."

"I know, but Dad," Olive pleaded, "remember what we were reading? Remember that there are a lot of handicapped people in some countries because of the wars? Don't you think a man who lost one leg might need it?"

Dad had to smile. "No, Olive. I don't think any charitable organization would even send it, and we're not going to drag the sandy thing back home."

Olive dropped the sandal and tagged behind the others. She forgot about it temporarily as they stopped to watch the sunset before leaving the trail. The sky above the ocean seemed to be on fire with streaks of brilliant color, and the whole party was silent for just a moment. Then Uncle Jim started singing "How Great Thou Art," and they all joined in. Olive sang with all her heart. The beautiful melody of the song and the gorgeous sunset fit together well.

Nobody felt like going home, but all good things come to an end, so everyone piled into the bus. Olive knew that Florence and Zachary were going to fall asleep soon, and Dad knew that too, because they decided to eat supper before they drove very far.

"Denny's has a deal right now where children eat free on Saturday nights," suggested Aunt Marge.

"We probably shouldn't take the time," Mom answered thoughtfully. "It's going to get late, so we should probably just pick up some fast food and keep moving."

"Oh, come on, Michelle," said Uncle Jim. "Marge is turning thirty only once in her life."

"You don't have to get a bunch of grouchy children ready for church in the morning," Mom told him, but Uncle Jim laughed.

"Don't worry about tomorrow," he said, and Olive hoped he could get Mom convinced. It would be much more fun to sit down at a restaurant than to eat in the bus.

After a long discussion, they really did go to Denny's. Olive couldn't believe it. What a perfect ending to a perfect day!

After everyone had eaten their fill, the crew headed back to the bus for the long ride home. The bus wheels hummed on and on as they traveled back to Frazier Park. Just when the children were getting bored, Uncle Jim lumbered back the aisle. "The old people are sleeping," he said. "Except your dad, of course."

"He'd better not be," said Leonard.

"Dad says he does sleep while he's driving sometimes," Tabitha informed Uncle Jim.

"Oh, yeah?" Olive could see that Uncle Jim didn't believe Tabitha.

"You see," Olive began. She thought she should explain it was a joke. "When Dad's sleepy, sometimes Mom offers to drive, and Dad says he can sleep better while he's driving than when Mom's driving."

Uncle Jim chuckled and dropped into the seat beside Leonard. It was dark outside, and it felt cozy to have Uncle Jim all to themselves. The children were quiet for a while. Suddenly Andrea piped up. "Uncle Jim, tell us a story."

"I think your mom probably told you all the stories I know," he said.

"We don't care," the children chorused, and Uncle Jim was quiet as he thought a little.

"Did your mom ever tell you about the time we went camping in British Columbia, way back in the bush?"

"She told us you went fishing in a little boat, and she threw her pole into the water when she was trying to cast her line."

"That's right," Uncle Jim said. "The boat almost tipped over, and your Uncle Joshua fell overboard."

"And he was thankful for his life jacket," added Olive.

"So," continued Uncle Jim, "I'll tell you something your mother didn't tell you about that camping trip. She didn't tell you because she didn't know it happened."

The children were all ears. What secret did Uncle Jim know?

"We went on a canoeing trip the second day," began Uncle Jim, and the children nodded. They knew that too.

"We crossed a lake in our canoes, which was easy as long as the water was calm and everyone worked together."

"And you saw a moose," added Madeline.

"Aha," Uncle Jim said, "you know part of the story. After we saw the moose, we were paddling back across the lake toward our cabin when a storm came up. It was pretty scary to be on that lake with that kind of waves. The park ranger had specifically told us to head to the nearest shore in the case of a thunderstorm.

"Well, your Uncle Merle was in the same canoe with me. He was eighteen and I was only thirteen, so it was comforting to have somebody older and more mature with me. But when the storm came up, Merle decided he'd better put on his life jacket, and he stopped paddling for a little. I felt our canoe turn sideways, and I knew if we didn't hit the waves head-on, we would capsize."

Olive held her breath. Surely they hadn't capsized, or Mom would have told them this part of the story.

Uncle Jim went on. "I was so scared we were going to flip the canoe that I cried. At age thirteen, I cried. And we didn't even tip. But Uncle Merle never told anyone what a big baby I was when I was scared. Now wasn't that a nice brother?"

"So there you are, Leonard," said Uncle Jim, thumping Leonard on the back. "You can take lessons from your Uncle Merle. He was a good brother. And now I think I'll go see if

Aunt Marge is awake and wants to talk to me a little."

It seemed darker after Uncle Jim left. The children balled their coats under their heads and tried to sleep.

Olive turned to Leonard. "That was a fun day," she said.

Leonard nodded. "It was. But I am dreading the end of the trail and all the sleeping and crying children."

"You need to be more like Uncle Jim," Olive told him. "He only worries about things as they come up."

"Maybe," said Leonard. "Want to see the shells I picked up?"

"I can't see them very well. It's too dark," Olive said. She curled up by the window. Pleasant memories of the day came rushing through her mind, and she fell asleep wondering how many handicapped people would have been happy for a sturdy sandal.

chapter four

"MAKE THEM BEHAVE," MOM SAID TO Aunt Marge. "And don't forget that Sandra needs a nap today."

Olive climbed into the tan maxi van with Mom and Andrea and baby Zachary. They were going to town. Leonard was spending the day with Dad, and the rest of the children were staying with Aunt Marge. Olive was glad it was her turn to go along to Bakersfield, but she would have rather gone with Dad. She had asked him if she could, but Dad had said no. He didn't think it was ladylike for his twelve-year-old daughter to be hanging around the jobsite where they were pouring concrete. Olive wanted to do just that. She loved to watch the gray, creamy concrete pour out of the truck. She liked taking a trowel and creating things with the pile of extra concrete that the truck drivers always dumped. Of course, it made her dirty, but what was wrong with a dirty girl? Why was that so much worse than a dirty boy? What she really wanted to do was to wear boots. Olive thought it would be fun to stomp around in the concrete like the men.

Why did she have to be a girl anyway? Dad had explained to her that God made both boys and girls special, but different, and the Bible made it clear that boys and girls had different responsibilities. Olive had often felt like a boy trapped in a girl's skin, but lately she had started to think being a girl wasn't so bad. Being a girl was great when it came to cooking. Boys could cook too, of course, and Leonard did sometimes, but it didn't come natural for him like it did for Olive.

Olive had to admit that there *was* something special about going to Bakersfield with Mom. Olive often mentioned that she liked a little peace and quiet now and then, and she was getting it now. The Brenneman house was often noisy, but now the van was quiet as they buzzed along. There was a little fog on the grapevine, which was what everybody called the road that passed through the mountains as it headed north from Los Angeles in the San Fernando Valley to Bakersfield in the San Joaquin Valley. The San Joaquin Valley was 250 miles long, and a lot of vegetables were grown there. That was the valley on the north side of the grapevine, and that's where they were headed now.

"Mom," Olive broke the silence, "why is this road called the grapevine?"

"I'm trying to remember," Mom said. She was passing

a car, and she had to focus on that for a little. When they were coasting along again, she looked at Olive and scratched her head. "Oh, yes, now I remember. This was a major highway in California since way back when Frazier Park was a gold-mining town. This road used to be called "The Ridge Route."

"So why is it called the grapevine now?"

"I'm coming to that," said Mom. "Along this difficult mountain pass there were lots of wild grapes growing, and that's how they identified the road. It was the one with the grapevines."

Frazier Park was the Brennemans' town, and it was situated at the top of the pass. Whenever they wanted to go to a larger city to shop, whichever direction they went, they had to drive down off the mountain on an eight-lane highway. Olive wondered what it would be like to live where Grandpa and Grandma did in Ohio and be only a few miles from the grocery store. You could step out your back door to get vegetables out of the garden. It seemed like a much better place to live. Why had Mom and Dad ever moved to southern California in the first place? Olive didn't even bother to ask Mom. She knew what Mom would say. They'd had this conversation many times. "It isn't about land," Mom would explain, "or we wouldn't be here. No, southern California isn't our dream place. But the people here need the Lord, and that's why we're here."

Olive knew Mom had struggled with moving to the desert in the first place. When Dad and Mom had told God that they would be willing to move to an area where the church needed families more than the big church back East did, Mom had been hoping to land up in the New England States or somewhere pretty. But Dad had reminded Mom that if you tell God you are willing to do the Lord's work in another area, you don't get out the map and give Him boundaries. Southern California needed committed Christians because there were a lot of truth seekers there, and Abram Miller felt God leading him to move there after realizing what a huge mission field it was.

"Mom," Olive asked suddenly, "did you ever see Alice and Mark Winton with red hair?"

"What in the world brought up that subject?" Mom asked.

"Well, I was just thinking about living in California, and I was thinking about when Abram Miller started this church. I remember you told me once that Alice and Mark sang in a rock band and had dyed their hair red before they found God. I just can't imagine them with red hair now!"

Mom's face was sober as she reflected on those first years. "No," she said. "Thankfully I never saw them with red hair myself, but Alice told me all about it. She told me how even after she and Mark found God, they tried to play in the rock band singing Christian songs. But finally they realized that Christians don't belong in rock bands.

"We visited Alice and Mark before this church was started," Mom said, "and they looked just as godly as they do today. But visiting with Mark and Alice was one thing that helped us to move to California, since they were begging for Christian fellowship. Of course Abram was glad for another family to join the small group here, and we've been happy here, don't you think?"

Olive nodded. It was true that the Brenneman family had learned to be at home in the "almost desert." People said it was beautiful, "in a way." Olive wasn't sure about it. It seemed much more beautiful back East where there were big red barns and milk cows in the pastures. She thought about the song, "Home on the Range," that Uncle Jim sometimes sang to them. The song talked about the beauty of the West "where the deer and the antelope play," but Olive didn't think the land where the deer and the antelope play was really beautiful at all.

* * * *

Mom drove down the mountain, flying past a lot of slow-moving tractor trailers. The trucks had to drive slowly so their brakes wouldn't overheat.

"Now get over where you belong, George," Mom said to the tractor trailer in front of her. "You're not supposed to be in this lane."

Olive laughed. Mom was learning. She used to call an unknown driver a "dude," but the children had told her they didn't think that was nice. From then on she used "George," like Dad did.

"Hey, I see a truck in the runaway truck ramp!" Andrea exclaimed. Olive checked it out as they whizzed by. It was always interesting to see how deep in the sand the wheels were. The tow truck was already there to get the truck out, and Olive guessed that the trucker was unhappy to lose his brakes and then have to pay all that money to get a tow truck. At least he was safe. Dad had once seen a truck lose its brakes close to Frazier Park, and it hadn't worked out so well for that driver. He had whizzed right down the exit ramp, through a Jack-in-the Box restaurant parking lot, and down a little hill where the truck burst into flames. The driver had burned up with the truck, and Dad had seen it all.

They were off the mountain now, and Mom was allowed to drive seventy miles per hour. It still seemed to take a long time until they got to town, but they arrived in Bakersfield just in time for Andrea's eye appointment. Olive hoped they wouldn't have to sit for two hours in the eye doctor's office like they did sometimes. Andrea had had regular eye appointments ever since she was little. She had been born cross-eyed and had to have surgery when she was one year old. Now the doctor still made her wear a patch on her good eye some of the time to keep the other one from becoming lazy.

It was lunchtime when they were done at the eye doctor's office, and Mom had many things to do in town. Things went well, though, and they were ready to head home by about suppertime. The back of the van was jammed with groceries. Mom called Dad on her cell phone to tell him that supper would be late, and then they were on their way. Mom glanced down at the gas gauge. "Olive, don't let me forget to get gas at the exit before the grapevine," she said. "We might have enough, but this old van's gas gauge goes down really fast at the end, so it's hard to tell."

Olive nodded. The van sure was a gas guzzler. Dad often wished he could get something that got better gas mileage, but vehicles that were not gas guzzlers were expensive, and Dad figured it would take a few years before the savings in gas would pay for a different vehicle. Sometimes he said they should just get a big RV to drive to town, and then they could fix their own food and use their own bathroom instead of making all those stops. Olive knew he was joking. An RV would take a lot of gas for sure. And imagine how hard it would be to park at Walmart!

The van was cozy and warm, and Olive soon fell asleep along with the baby and Andrea. Suddenly she woke up to Mom's concerned voice. "What is wrong with this van?" There was just enough space between cars for Mom to coast across two lanes and get off the edge of the road.

Olive assessed the situation. They were part-way up the grapevine. "You ran out of gas," she said.

"That is right!" said Mom in alarm. "Now here we are, way out in Timbuktu, and my cell phone battery died right after I called Dad."

Olive looked at Mom, and Mom looked at Olive. "We'll just sit here for a while. Maybe someone will stop and help us," Mom decided.

Olive sat quietly. She was scared. *God knows we're here*, she thought. *I'd better ask Him to help us.* After she prayed, she felt better. Someone would stop.

But no one did.

"I've been praying," she told Mom.

"Believe me, I have been too," Mom said, "But I wonder how long we should sit here. I mean, it's dangerous to sit on the shoulder of an eight-lane highway where people are rushing by at sixty-five miles an hour. Maybe I should pop up the hood to show people that we have trouble."

"Maybe." Olive wasn't too sure that would help because people regularly stopped along the grapevine to cool off their engines. Besides, almost everyone had a cell phone, and everyone expected you to have one too.

Mom got out and put up the hood of the van, but still no one stopped. Olive was tempted to get mad at all those people sailing by. Didn't they see that this van needed help?

For a while Olive looked at the cars whizzing by and imagined where the people were going. She pictured them all going home to their families, and she imagined what kind of houses they lived in. If they drove old, beat-up cars, she pictured old, dilapidated houses. If they were driving nice, new vehicles, she envisioned the mansions they must be going home to.

Andrea and Zachary were still sleeping, but Mom decided to wake Andrea. "We can't sit here forever," she said, "and Dad is going to get worried soon." Mom thought for a little. "I don't think the exit at the bottom of the grapevine is more than a mile away, so I guess we'll just have to walk. My dad did that many a time when he ran out of gas."

Mom woke Andrea and explained the situation to her. "Where will we walk?" Andrea asked. "What if the cars hit us?"

Mom shook her head. "I don't think they will. We'll walk on the other side of the guard rail."

"But Mom," Olive wailed, "this road is on the side of the mountain. In some places a steep bank is next to the guard rail."

"I know, but there will surely be a foot or two where we can walk," Mom replied.

They began to walk slowly beside the guard rail: Mom, Olive, and Andrea. Mom was carrying Zachary, who was still sleeping. Andrea had a sweater, but Olive didn't, and it was chilly. Mom didn't have one either, but she had a nice thick blanket on Zachary, which helped her out too.

They hadn't walked very far before it began to get dusky. Olive shivered. "Mom, I'm cold," she complained.

"I know, Olive, but you'll have to be brave. This is a good lesson for us to dress for the weather because we never know what will happen."

"When will we get there?" Andrea asked.

"Please, Andrea," Mom said. "It will be a long walk, and you must just walk in front of me nicely. Not everything is pleasant in life, and we just have to do what we have to do."

The briars pulled at their dresses, and the wind stirred up by the passing cars blew their hair, but they kept walking. Suddenly the bank dropped steeply, just as Olive had feared. Mom clutched Zachary tighter, and they walked single file right beside the guard rail. By then it was completely dark. They could see to walk only by the light from the oncoming headlights.

"Just think," Mom said. "What if we were in a country without religious freedom and we'd be fleeing from our persecutors. Wouldn't that be scary?"

Olive thought about that for a few minutes, and then she felt more peaceful. They weren't in another country, and they had only run out of gas. No matter what the next hour held, she had confidence that they would get help somewhere. Olive did wonder what all the people driving by them thought—one woman with a head-covering and a long dress holding a baby and followed by two girls, walking along the highway in the darkness. Maybe people would really think they had escaped from somewhere.

It seemed they had walked for a long time when a car with flashing lights pulled up in front of them. It was a policeman, and Olive breathed a great sigh of relief. Surely they could stop walking, and the policeman would take care of them.

Mom was telling the policeman what had happened. "I just need to call my husband for a ride," she explained.

The policeman was all business. "You need to get off the road," he said. They climbed into the back of the police car. The seats were hard plastic, and there were metal bars to divide the front of the car from the back. *This is where criminals ride,* Olive realized. *I doubt they feel relieved like I do.*

Mom used the policeman's phone and called Dad. There

was a restaurant at the grapevine exit, and Dad said he would pick them up there. It wasn't late enough that Dad had been seriously worried, but he had started to wonder why they weren't home.

"How were you going to cross to the other side of the divided highway?" the policeman asked Mom as he drove them toward the restaurant.

"I figured we'd cross that bridge when we got to it," Mom answered a little sheepishly. "Isn't there a road under the highway?"

"Actually there is," the policeman acknowledged.

Olive wondered if the policeman was impressed that Mom had decided to do something about her plight, or if he thought she was a little crazy for trying such a thing in the pitch black night. Of course, policemen don't usually tell you what they're thinking, so Olive was left to wonder.

The policeman dropped them off at the restaurant, and they sat on benches inside to wait on Dad. After Mom had explained to the cashier what had happened, the cashier brought them each a little bag of teddy grahams to eat. Zachary had slept the whole time they were walking, but now he peeked his head out of his blanket and ate teddy grahams. Olive wasn't even hungry. She hadn't realized how worked up she had been about the whole ordeal.

Dad had never seemed so much like a knight in shining armor as he did that night when he walked in the door of the restaurant. It felt so good to all ride in the car together. But then they had to stop at the gas station to buy some gas for the van and get that going. After that they had to pick up the children who had stayed with Aunt Marge, and of course, they had to tell her the story. So it was bedtime until they got home. Even so, they all stayed up a while and discussed the event some more.

"I didn't know which was more dangerous," Mom told Dad, "staying in the van on the shoulder or walking outside the guard rail. The policeman did say that quite a few people had called in, so I suppose we should have just stayed in the van."

"You never know, though," Dad said. "Maybe they wouldn't have called if they just saw a van with problems. But when they see a mother with three children walking, well, that's just not something you see every day."

"I suppose we did look a sight," Mom admitted, "but I'm thankful for so many things. I'm so glad Zachary was sleeping, and I'm thankful for the light from the headlights, and most of all, I'm thankful for the trustworthy policeman who rescued us! God did take care of us, even if we had to work a little."

"We knew He would," said Olive, "and anyway, we learned not to take chances with the gas tank in the van."

"That's for sure," Mom laughed. "I totally forgot about it until the van acted funny. Oh, well, some of us have to learn the hard way!"

Olive lay in bed and thought about it. Had God really heard them praying? If He had, why didn't anybody stop? Of course, the policeman had stopped to pick them up, but that didn't really seem like a miracle, seeing they had to walk so far in the dark. *I guess everything can't be perfect for Christians*, she thought. *The Anabaptists were beheaded, and God allowed that.*

Olive again thought about Ohio. Somehow life there seemed so much easier and less stressful. Maybe they should just move back there. But then she thought of Uncle Craig's family and Uncle Jim and Aunt Marge. She wouldn't want to leave them. And then there was Doug Remington and the other community people. Who would show them the way if Christians weren't willing to live in Frazier Park, California?

chapter five

THE TRACTOR TRAILER PULLED OUT OF Grandpa's lane, and the Brenneman family was headed back to California. No one driving past them would have guessed that packed inside the sleeper of the truck were eight children—two boys and six girls.

The Brennemans had hauled a load of oranges from Luke Reber's orange grove back to the East. Luke Reber's family had been the first family to move to California when the church started, and they lived in Bakersfield. Since they were the only ones in the church who lived in the valley, they were the only ones who could grow oranges. Luke was glad when the church men would drive his truck east, and the Brennemans were glad for a free trip to Ohio. They had first dropped off oranges in Colorado, and then there had been many other stops the whole way to Ohio.

Olive was excited to travel in the truck again on the way

home, yet she knew she would get tired of it by the time they got back to California. On the way to Ohio it had been fun for the first few days, but after that, it had seemed like two million miles to Grandpa's house, instead of two thousand. Now the excitement of being with their relatives was past, and they faced the long road home.

The one thing that had broken the monotony on the way to Ohio had been the meals. The macaroni and cheese and the greasy fried chicken from the truck stops tasted wonderful to the children. They had eventually gotten tired of it, but after the two-week break at Grandpa's place, Olive was ready to eat some greasy food at a truck stop again. It was fun, too, to see the other truckers' eyes get big when all the Brennemans tumbled out of the truck. The truckers were used to seeing men in T-shirts and cowboy boots, not families packed into a sleeper like a new pack of pencils.

"At least the trip home should go faster—don't you think we should be able to make it in four days?" Mom asked Dad hopefully.

"I wouldn't bank on it," he said while shifting gears. "Truck driving can be pretty maddening if you're trying to make time. We've got to drop off this load and pick up another one, you know."

"Well, surely one load won't throw us off too much." Mom glanced back at the two youngest children who were already sleeping.

Olive lay down on the bed and tried to take a nap too. Her mind was filled with so many happy memories of Ohio that they chased each other all over her brain till they were only a muddle. She began to sort them out.

There was the safari that Grandpa and Grandma took them to, along with Uncle Mike and Aunt Cathy and the Brenneman cousins. They got to ride in an old bus to see the animals, and it was fun, even if it had rained. Olive and her siblings thought the rain was neat, because in California it rarely rained in the summer. They were worried about getting raindrops on their shoes until Dad informed them that it rained year-round in Ohio, and a little water wouldn't hurt their shoes.

Two days later Grandpa and Grandma Birky and Uncle Conrad, who was still living at home, had taken them to an old-fashioned village. Uncle Joshua's family had gone along too. Uncle Joshua's children were still pretty young, so Olive didn't have anyone her age to be with, but it was still great fun to see the village and listen to Uncle Joshua and Mom talk about when they had been young.

Uncle Joshua was a school teacher now, and Olive could hardly believe he had ever been so immature. Now it seemed that he knew a little about everything, but his favorite hobby was taking care of bees. Uncle Joshua could tell you all about bees, and he loved to eat honey.

Then there was the fishing. Uncle Conrad took them to a pond to go fishing, and Leonard and Olive had loved that the most. There were hardly any ponds and lakes close to their home in Frazier Park, and the few that were fairly close were usually crowded with people from Los Angeles who wanted to get out of the city for a while. Close to Grandpa's house in Ohio, though, there were all kinds of ponds to fish in.

There were also creeks. Mom talked about visiting her friends' houses when she was little, and it seemed that everyone had a swimming hole in their cow pasture. Grandpa Brenneman's farm had one too, so Dad had grown up with one. He talked about the wild mint tea that grew along the banks of the creek. It was so abundant that, at a certain time of the year, the cows' milk would taste of mint because they grazed on it.

One day the Brenneman girls went shopping with Mom, Grandma, and Great-Grandma in Amish Country. There were orderly fabric shops and bulk food stores, and, along the way, the children watched the Amish pitch hay onto their wagons and drive their horses in the fields.

"I can't believe I'm staring at those Amish," Mom had laughed at herself. "When I was young, we used to get tired of the tourists driving slowly to look at these "quaint" people. Now here I am, doing it myself. I've been away from it so long that I feel kind of like a tourist myself. It really is picturesque."

"I'm guessing the people in southern California feel the same about you," Great-Grandma had added, and Mom had to agree.

Olive fell asleep in the middle of her reminiscing, and when she woke up, Mom was feeding the children some lunch. Olive was glad Grandma had packed lunch for them. What was truck stop food compared to Grandma's sweet bologna sandwiches on her homemade white bread? And Swiss cheese! Olive loved Swiss cheese. She took her sandwich apart to check how many holes were in her slice of cheese and felt a bit let down to see that there were only two in her entire piece.

"Leonard, let's start a cheese factory when we grow up," Olive suggested out of the blue. Leonard swallowed his bite and stared at her.

"Do you have any idea how to make it?"

"Not really, but if the people in Ohio can make it, then I'm sure I can."

Leonard shook his head. "What happened to your practical plan of adopting orphans?"

"Well, I decided I might get married after all. So I will need a job until then."

"Better wait and see if someone wants to marry a cheese maker," Leonard said, and Olive threw a cracker at his head. Leonard calmly caught it and ate it.

Olive went back to her sandwich. *So much for his input.* Leonard was a good brother, but sometimes it was exasperating to have a brother who thought in neat, square boxes.

"So where do we drop our load of feed?" Mom asked Dad.

"Nebraska. We should be there tomorrow morning."

"And then?"

"We have to pick up eggs. That's in Nebraska too, but a

few hours farther west."

It was nine o'clock the second day when the truck pulled into the small town in Nebraska where they were supposed to drop off the feed. Dad was on the phone.

"You say turn onto Elm Street and drive just out of town? Alrighty, that's what I will do." Dad flipped his cell phone shut and put it in his pocket.

"Sounds a little sketchy," he said to no one in particular. "I guess the farmers just meet us there."

Olive and Leonard peered out the back windows of the sleeper. Madeline, Tabitha, and Andrea were peeking around Mom's and Dad's seats, trying to see where they were. Was the countryside still green, or had they reached a dry area where things had to be irrigated?

"Oh, this is a cute little town!" Mom exclaimed. "It looks like a place where everyone knows everyone else."

Dad scratched his head. "Elm Street. Where is it? There seems to be only one main road. Oh, here it is—just a little side street."

It took a little maneuvering to get the truck and trailer turned in, but Dad had once been a truck driver in farming country. He had needed to back in and out of farmers' fields for years, so he was able to make the turn without much trouble. He stopped just past the last house. At first there didn't seem to be anyone there to greet them. But very soon a white pickup truck appeared with a fiftyish-looking farmer in striped overalls. In about ten minutes, five more pickups showed up with farmers who needed feed for their cows. Leonard jumped out to help, and Mom decided to take the girls on a walk.

It was a beautiful day in Nebraska. They walked down the road beside the farmers' lush green fields. It felt so good to take a country walk after being cooped up in the truck for a day and a half.

When they got back to the truck, the farmers were still unloading the bags by hand. Olive stood by the truck and watched. The farmers were joking and talking as if they were all old friends. They were regular hardworking farmers. Olive drank it all in. She hoped she would marry a farmer some day. Mom had always said that too when she was a little girl, and she did marry a farm boy, but then he decided not to be a farmer. Well, as much as she loved Dad just the way he was, Olive hoped she could be a little more successful than that.

Dad was hoping to be at the next stop by lunchtime that day, and he wanted to get in the ten hours of driving time that his driver's log allowed. But it was a little later than he planned when they finally spotted the egg factory. And that's what it was! Fourteen chicken houses stood in a row, with one big building that was obviously the packing plant.

"What kind of eggs will we get?" asked three-year-old Florence.

"Regular eggs, silly," Tabitha told her.

Florence frowned. "I wanted pickled eggs."

The whole Brenneman family was laughing as they pulled into the factory. Dad went in to talk to the managers, and soon he came back with bad news.

"I hate to tell you, but they have to package the eggs yet."

"You mean they have to put them on pallets," Mom said confidently.

"No. I mean the eggs are just now being brought from the chicken house."

Olive and Leonard both groaned in unison. "I hope the eggs are coming in at about twenty miles an hour," Leonard said. "I hope it's all done by a machine."

"I'm afraid it would take Dr. Seuss to invent a machine like that," Dad smiled. "This is the life of a trucker. Patience." He went into the building to wait, and the rest of the family felt depressed.

Mom tried to be upbeat. "Shall I tell you a story while we wait? The chicken houses reminded me of something from my childhood."

Of course the children wanted to hear a story, so Mom began: "My grandma, your Grandpa Birky's mother, died when I was eight. She had been bedfast for a long time, so in a way it was not sad when she died. She could stop suffering and go to heaven. But I loved Grandma—I made her cards, and she would tell me how beautiful they were and what an artist I was!"

"No wonder you liked her," said Leonard.

Mom laughed. "Of course, all children like to be noticed by adults, and Grandma did have a way of making me feel special. We used to visit her one evening a week to help Grandpa take care of her, and then we would sing for her before we went home. Your uncles, Joshua and Jim, were just little boys, and Grandma liked when they sang for her."

"You mean Uncle Jim who lives close to us?" Andrea asked.

"That same Uncle Jim," Mom nodded. "Can you imagine him as a little boy?"

Andrea shook her head solemnly, but Mom went on. "And then Grandma would always ask my parents, your Grandpa and Grandma Birky, to sing 'Angels Rock Me to Sleep' before we left. Then we would make the half-hour drive home. We thought that was a long way."

"Ha," Olive laughed. "That's not very far. We drive farther than that to go to town."

"But it was long for us," said Mom. "Well, my grandma died, and we went to the viewing. The family got there early to see Grandma before anyone else came. I remember looking at Grandma in the casket, and she didn't really look like Grandma. My Aunt Lois said her hair wasn't combed right, so maybe that was why. It was strange to see the aunts crying, but they didn't cry long, because, as I said, it really was a happy thing that she could go to heaven.

"Then other people started pouring in, and I wondered how I was supposed to act. Nobody I knew well had ever died before. I watched my aunts. They had wads of tissues in their hands, and now and then they would wipe their eyes. I wished I could cry so everyone would see how sad I was and how much I loved my grandma, so I went to the restroom to get some tissues. I tried to look sad, and I wiped my eyes now and then."

"Mom, did you really do that?" Madeline asked. "That was acting a lie, wasn't it?"

"Well," said Mom, "acting a lie is purposely trying to deceive someone, and I was trying really hard to cry. I had convinced myself that I might need those tissues. But it got boring, trying to cry, and so my cousin Abigail and I just walked around looking at people. Finally Aunt Shirley came to our rescue. She had to go home to do chores, and she wondered if Abigail and I wanted to go along. Of course, we said yes. And Aunt Shirley had a chicken house."

"So that's why these chicken houses reminded you of this story," Olive interrupted.

"Yes," Mom replied before continuing with the story. "Our parents agreed that we could go, and so we walked to Aunt Shirley's house, which was just down the road. Aunt Shirley found some old dresses from her daughter who was all grown up, and we went out to the chicken house. It was a lot of fun watching Aunt Shirley gather the eggs. In the background we could hear the excited chickens, but the egg-packing room was quiet.

"The eggs rolled down a belt from the part of the building where the chickens were. In the corner of the packing room was a little black closed-off area where a person stood to check the eggs for cracks. The eggs went past a little light, and if there were cracks in the eggs, the light would show the cracks. Then the good eggs moved on, and someone put them in flats. We stood and watched for a long time. Every once in a while an egg got smashed, and the gooey yellow would run onto the floor.

"We had the funeral for Grandma the next day," Mom continued. "It was bitterly cold. I sat beside my dad, and he didn't cry at all. He told Mom later that he just couldn't feel sad enough to cry. He said Grandma was in a better place, and he wouldn't have wanted her to have to lie in bed for years and years. I couldn't understand what the preacher was saying, but it was a lot about heaven.

"After the service, we filed out to the graveyard. There was a big hole dug for Grandma, and I watched in awe as they lowered Grandma in there. I was truly sad, and I wished some tears would have come, but I was as dry-eyed as ever.

"After that we all went home, and Grandpa went home to an empty house. He was used to feeding and taking care of Grandma all the time, so it was hard for him to be so lonely. We still visited him pretty often and tried to keep him company."

The little children had fallen asleep by now, but they woke up again when Dad finally came out to give them an update on the progress. Mom asked him if there was a restroom inside.

"Sure, come in," Dad said. "Maybe they'll let you watch them pack the eggs."

After they used the restroom, the manager pointed out a break room with a glass window through which they could watch the packing machines. Dad herded them all inside, and there they sat. To Olive's surprise, the workers were almost all Hispanics. She had thought California was the only state that had Hispanic workers.

The Brennemans were hungry. Mom had given them a few snacks midmorning, but she was hoping they could buy a decent meal at lunch time. But there weren't any truck stops around this primitive area, so they had snacked a little more and called it lunch. But after watching the packers for a few more hours, the children were getting tired, grouchy, and hungry.

Suddenly, who came into the break room, but a short, round lady with her hands full of Mexican food? What a smell! And what was more amazing yet, she was offering the food to Dad. She couldn't talk more than a few words of English, but with what she did know and some hand gestures, Dad understood that she sold food to the workers. She motioned that he could buy some too. Dad bought four plates of food for them to share.

Next, the lady pulled out some large Styrofoam cups and poured juice into them. The juice tasted like liquid sugar. It was so sweet! There was a vending machine in the break room, and Dad bought some 7 Up to mix with the juice. It cut the sweetness and added some fizz to the delicious melon flavor. The children polished off the rice and beans while Mom and Dad ate the chili rellenos, which were breaded, deep-fried chili peppers stuffed with Mexican cheese.

It was almost evening when the manager finally told Dad that the truck was loaded. The Brennemans didn't have to be told twice. They boarded the truck once more to continue their journey to California.

"My, that's hard to take when I want to get home so badly," Dad said as they pulled onto the highway. "But, you know, there are a lot of things to be thankful for. Just when we were getting terribly bored and hungry, God sent that lady to help us out."

"It was interesting to watch them pack eggs," added Leonard.

"See?" said Dad. "Who needs a school field trip? You children got two already today. You know what small-town Nebraska looks like, and you know a *lot* about commercial poultry farms."

Dad drove long into the night, and the next morning they got up as early as his log book would let him. Olive was bored stiff. She was so ready to get home! But Dad had said that in the afternoon they would cross the Colorado Rockies, and she was looking forward to that.

Just when the children were so tired of traveling that all they could seem to do was fight, they started getting into the mountains and snow. "I have a feeling we'd better get a motel," said Dad. "I don't have chains for my tires, and that sign says we have to have them to travel tonight. Besides," he continued, "I've got eggs. I don't think they'll handle a wreck very well."

"Don't you care about us?" Madeline asked, and Dad laughed as he reached behind his seat and tweaked her ear.

"Of course I do. But are my children as fragile as eggs?"

"We aren't going to make it home until late tomorrow evening, anyway," Mom said with resignation. "We might as well take our time. Isn't it funny how we look forward to a trip so much, but when we're almost home, we are more excited than when we left?"

It was afternoon the next day before the scenery started looking like they were close to home. They passed through Las Vegas. Dad always said that he didn't look to the right or the left more than necessary when he went through that city because of all the evil things there. Olive did look to the left because that was the only window she could see out of in the sleeper. She saw the high glitzy buildings and the advertisements for casinos, and she wondered how people could go in those doors and waste their hard-earned money.

The miles flew by as they crossed the desert. They were almost at the California state line. Then they'd travel through more desert until they hit the mountains of home.

"Mom," Olive said suddenly, "why do we live out here? I mean, isn't it so much nicer in Ohio? You could grow a garden there, and we could have a grassy yard to play in."

Mom thought for a minute. "Remember, Olive, if it were about land, we probably wouldn't live here. We moved out here to help people learn about the Bible, and think of all the people who have come to church. Which reminds me," Mom said, looking at Dad, "Aunt Marge says there's a boy from Los Angeles who's been coming to church. He grew up in Eli Glick's church in El Salvador."

"That's interesting," replied Dad. "I wonder how he got

to the States and why he ended up in Los Angeles."

"Marge says he was disobedient to his parents and the church and ran away from home to come to the States, but now he's repented and wants to visit a church that he feels teaches the truth."

"Well, praise the Lord!" said Dad. "I hope we can be a family to him, and I hope he sincerely wants to do what is right."

"Anyway," said Mom, looking at Olive, "anywhere you live, helping people to the Lord is what makes life truly satisfying. And we've learned to feel at home in California, don't you think?"

"I guess, but it's so fun at Grandpa's house."

"That isn't real life, Olive. Do you know that your cousins get tired of mowing the grass and doing their farm chores? They would love to come see the things that our life holds in California."

"Like what?"

"Like the ocean and lizards and big cities and wildfires."

"And bears," added Leonard.

"And snakes," added Andrea.

Olive thought about it. Those were things she took for granted. They did make life interesting, she had to admit. But Mom wasn't done.

"I sometimes get homesick for some of those things in Ohio too," she admitted. "But you know, Olive, we wouldn't be happy there if we knew God wanted us in California, helping the people here. Wherever God wants us is where we want to feel at home."

As Dad pulled into the truck stop a few miles from home, they saw their familiar maxi van waiting to take them up the mountain, and a warm, homey feeling came over Olive. It felt so good to come back to familiar territory, and as the lights of home came into view, she knew that Mom was right. It was good to be home.

chapter six

"CAN WE FIT?" LEONARD ASKED AS DAD carefully maneuvered the van into the church parking lot. Olive let out her breath as Dad pulled into the parking spot. It was difficult to get many vehicles parked in front of their church. Lebec Christian Fellowship met in a four-car garage connected to a double-wide trailer. The driveway was small, and people had to park tightly to fit into the driveway.

The double-wide trailer itself was what the church people called the "mission house," and in the early days, the church people had built the garage onto the trailer to use as their auditorium for church services. Olive didn't remember it, but her family had taken their turn living at the mission house when they had first moved into the area ten years before. The neighbor man had once called the Mennonites a "bunch of gypsies," since people were always moving in and out of the mission house. It was a house for any of the church families who needed temporary housing, or sometimes for a neighbor family who was down and out. Right now it was empty, and it was a good place for the children to play after church.

"Looks like we have some visitors," Dad commented as they climbed out. They all looked at the beat-up pickup truck sitting at the end of the row of cars. There was a car with Pennsylvania plates too—maybe some relatives of one of the church members.

After the Brennemans were all sitting at their places in church, Olive peeked over her shoulder. She had gotten a glimpse of the local visitor when she came in, and she thought he was worthy of another. Mom frowned at her, and Olive quickly turned to face the song leader. Her second glance had been long enough to see the man though. He had long, untrimmed hair and a shaggy mustache. The little girls kept looking around, and Mom was kept busy trying to interest them in singing.

Olive searched the small crowd for the Pennsylvania folks, and sure enough, she saw a young woman on the women's side and a young man on the men's side who fit together pretty well. They were almost certainly on their honeymoon. Lots of honeymooning couples stopped by their church, and Dad and Mom loved to find out who they were and see if they could make a connection. Usually they could—either they knew an uncle, or went to Bible School with a friend . . . or something.

Tim Blake got up to moderate the service, and he was

muttering something as he walked up front. Olive strained to hear him. Tim was a stern-looking man who had been in the military for many years. At first you were scared of him, until you learned that it was all bluff. Tim was as soft-hearted a man as you would find, and he was always muttering. The Brenneman children had found out that if you listened closely to his muttering, sometimes you could hear some really funny things. Sometimes he started his introduction to the service by heaving a great sigh and saying, "What a morning!" This morning, though, he only greeted the visitors and went on with the service as normal.

As the service progressed, Olive noticed that Bob Julian was there and that he was extra talkative. Once more she wondered where he had come from. He had called their minister, Abram Miller, one day and asked to be picked up at the local truck stop. He had said he was a Christian Jew and that he had escaped from the military in Israel. He had told Abram that his real name wasn't Bob Julian, but that was the only name he would give. He lived in a travel trailer someone had provided for him on the church grounds, and he loved to talk in Sunday school.

More and more, the church people were wondering what his real story was. He seemed very American and knew all about American politics. He told lots of big stories about his family in Israel, but they were all very general and didn't seem believable. Was this man hiding from someone? No one knew.

Olive knew Mom and Dad didn't really believe his story,

and Mom worried a little about the church people having him over for meals and social events. But Dad didn't see what harm could come from giving someone meals once a week, even if his stories didn't match up. "We need to take care of visitors who drop in," he had said. "You never know when they might be angels unawares."

"I hardly think an angel would say things that aren't true," Mom had answered, but she kept being friendly to Bob and inviting him over.

Well, if Olive thought Bob Julian told tall tales, the new visitor had him beat. After church, he had the men gathered around him, and he was talking. His name was Jim, and he was a welder, he said. If the men had any welding jobs, they could hire him. He owned a big ranch a half-hour's drive away, and if he sold it, he would be a millionaire.

Not long after the church service, preacher Abram asked the men if they wanted to hold a street meeting that afternoon.

All the men nodded their heads, as Olive hoped they would. Lebec Christian Fellowship had not had a street meeting for a long, long time, and Olive wanted to see downtown Los Angeles. She had never been there, except to drive through on the freeway. Dad's banker from Ohio had warned him about moving so close to a big city like Los Angeles. "It's like living in Sodom and Gomorrah," he had said. He hadn't known that they would be living in the country, up in the mountains away from the skyscrapers and the smog.

Once, the church had gone to Hollywood Boulevard for a street meeting. Olive hadn't gone along, but the report from the people who went had been fascinating. "Movie stars do radical things to get attention," they had said. "But all you have to do to get more attention is wear long dresses and head coverings or plain old pants and shirts. Someone even took a video of us."

After the service, preacher Abram and the brethren discussed where to have the street meeting. Some of the men weren't too sure about Hollywood Boulevard. They felt more as if they were being a spectacle for curious onlookers than really being a witness, and they weren't too sure about taking their families to where so many wicked sights were to be seen.

Tim Blake had another idea. He had grown up in a suburb of Los Angeles, and he knew of an outdoor mall where you could hold events like street meetings. It was called Santa Monica Mall. Everyone agreed with this idea. It seemed like the right place to go. Olive was slightly disappointed because she really had wanted to see Hollywood, but surely Santa Monica Mall would be interesting too.

Leonard wanted to go along for the street meeting as much as Olive did, and they were thrilled when Mom and Dad gave their permission. Preacher Abram's wife and daughters were going to stay home and babysit all the little children so the parents and older children would be able to go along.

After lunch, the group piled into vans, and before long

the green, grass-covered hills were whizzing by. The hills turned into flat, rocky desert, and Olive fell asleep for a few minutes as they drove. When she awoke, she could see skyscrapers in the distance, and the men were talking about earthquakes.

"You wouldn't want to be here when these buildings started to topple," one of them mentioned. Olive shivered. She hadn't thought of that danger. But when Dad spoke, she was comforted.

"I read somewhere that they have experimented with putting these huge buildings on gigantic rollers so that when they get shaken by an earthquake, they just give. I think the article said it had worked pretty well."

They all agreed it was a smart idea, and Olive hoped they were all built that way by now. It was good Tim Blake was driving the lead van, because he knew just where to go. They kept turning corners around the tall buildings until they entered a parking garage.

Olive was excited as they climbed out of the vans and started walking down the street. "I wonder what Grandpa and Grandma would say if they would see us now," she said to Leonard.

"Or the banker," Leonard said, grinning in a way that Olive knew he thought it was exciting too.

They climbed some stairs that led to a huge shopping center. It felt strange to be in a shopping mall on Sunday, but soon they went out the back door to the outside part of the mall. Here the streets had been blocked off to traffic and turned into an outdoor marketplace.

The group strolled down the middle of the streets, which were lined with people selling their wares or entertaining the crowds. The first thing that caught Olive's attention was a little boy who was dancing. He had a sound system that boomed out the music as he sang into his microphone and danced to the rhythm. He had a plastic container beside him, and some people would stop to listen and then drop a dollar or two into the container.

Just as Olive was thinking that he was making money pretty fast, her attention was drawn to a group of three African-American men standing along the street. They were dressed in traditional African clothes, handing out papers. They gave one to Dad as he walked by. Dad read it as he walked and explained what the mission of the three men was. "They claim to belong to the lost tribes of the children of Israel," he said. "Did you notice the painting beside them of an African-looking man? That's their picture of Jesus."

As they walked, Olive tried to remember all the different things they were seeing so that she could tell Madeline and the rest. Suddenly she saw something that she would have no trouble remembering. Standing ahead of them in the middle of the street was a silver man. The whole group had stopped to watch him a little. Was he real? He looked just like a statue; everything from head to toe, including his hair, was shining silver. If you looked closely, though, you could see his eyes move, and every now and then he moved his hand and shook some coins he had in a little silver can. He was collecting money from the people who walked past! As fascinating as it was to Olive, she thought how uncomfortable it must be to be stiff with paint all day, and she wondered how he got it off.

The group moved on, and Olive moved too. Somehow it didn't seem like a good place to get separated from her parents. The next thing she knew, Tim Blake was telling everybody to stop and get their songbooks. Olive had seen one more thing she wondered about, though, and she whispered to Leonard, "What is wrong with that man over there? It looks like he's talking to the light pole."

Leonard shook his head, but Tim had overheard her. In low tones he explained. "That man is hallucinating. He has taken drugs too much of his life, and it has ruined his brain. He really thinks that light pole is a person."

Olive looked at the man with amazement. Sure enough, while she watched, he shook his finger at the light pole, and a new batch of words burst from his lips. As the group began to sing, Olive thought about how many people they were singing to who had never heard songs about Jesus. It made her feel good to think that maybe they could help someone be saved from a life that would end in drugs and talking to light poles!

As they sang, some people stopped to listen. Usually they listened for a minute and walked on. Olive wondered what was going through their minds. Did the songs trigger a memory—maybe the faith of a mother or grandmother? Or did they put the church from Lebec in the same category as the silver man? Did they just think the Mennonites were people who wanted to attract attention?

After they sang a while, preacher Abram asked Dad and Mom if they wanted to pass out some tracts and take Olive and Leonard along. Dad picked up a stack of tracts, and together they walked down the street. Olive was disappointed that the singing couldn't be heard better from a distance. There was just too much noise.

After a bit, Dad and Leonard walked to the other side of the street to pass out tracts, and Mom and Olive stayed where they were. "Would you like to read some good news?" Mom asked the people passing by. Some people took the tracts and thanked her, but a lot just shook their heads and kept walking.

A couple girls walked by, and Mom offered them a tract. "Who are you?" one girl asked.

"We're Christians. We believe the Bible," Mom answered. Then she asked, "Are you familiar with the Bible?" The young girl shook her head and rejected the tract.

Soon some older ladies walked by. Mom offered them tracts, and they all shook their heads. They didn't seem friendly at all. The one glanced up and said, "We're Jews." Mom didn't know what to say, and the ladies walked on. Olive was surprised. It seemed like Jews should believe the Bible, but she remembered that most Jews didn't believe that Jesus was God's Son, so of course they wanted nothing to do with Christianity. They believed only the Old Testament.

When their stack of tracts was gone, the Brennemans

headed back to the group and again joined in singing. As they sang, Olive noticed a young woman sitting on the curb, listening. She had her hands over her face, and she appeared to be crying. "Should I go talk to her?" Olive heard Mom say to Dad.

"Whatever you think," Dad said. "It does seem like someone should."

In a few minutes Mom walked over to the lady and sat beside her. She didn't notice that Mom was there. Finally Mom tapped her on the shoulder. The lady jumped and looked up. "Is there something I can help you with?" Mom asked.

"Oh, no," the lady said quickly. "It's just that my children have been acting awful today."

"Oh, I'm sorry about that," Mom said and waited quietly, wanting to give the lady a chance to talk. She didn't seem interested, so Mom returned to the group. But in a few minutes, Mom had a surprise. The lady rounded up her two children and walked across the street. She walked up to Mom and gave her a big hug. She thanked her for caring. Then she was gone.

As the group walked back to the van, Olive felt like she had seen so many things that she was almost dizzy. She certainly did have a lot to tell the other girls.

That evening the Brennemans all sat around the table eating supper and talking about their afternoon.

"Well, that surely was interesting," Mom said. "It makes you feel good to make contact with people in the city and try to make a little bit of a difference."

"It sure feels like they put us on the 'different planet' shelf, though," Dad commented.

Mom thought a minute. "In a sense we are," she said. "We belong to the 'New Kingdom' planet. We don't really want to fit into Los Angeles, California."

"The lost tribes of the children of Israel didn't either," Leonard remarked, and Dad had to laugh.

"You're right there," he agreed.

"But we're not trying to be different just for the sake of being different," Dad went on. "A Christian should live the life God wants him to, and if that makes him different, then that's fine. But we don't need to take a bath in silver so that everyone notices us and knows we're different."

"Do you think Los Angeles is like Sodom and Gomorrah in the Bible?" Olive asked.

Dad laid down his spoon before he answered. "It seems like Sodom and Gomorrah couldn't have been much worse. I do admire the brave souls who live in Los Angeles and try to make a difference by preaching the Gospel. But we have to be careful wherever we live in this wicked world, that we don't feel at home, as Lot seemed to feel in Sodom.

"I have to say," said Dad, looking at Leonard, "this was a different Sunday afternoon then I ever had when I was a boy."

"What were your Sunday afternoons like?" Andrea asked.

"Yes, tell us," Madeline agreed.

"Well, for starters, at our house we had to do farm

chores," Dad began. "So we didn't have a lot of free time in the afternoons. We would eat a big lunch of ham or poor man's steak, and then we would go on bike rides or read books or just be lazy. We didn't take naps though. Why Mom and Dad would want to sleep on Sunday afternoons was beyond us! And in the evening, after we did our chores, we would often go visit an older person or someone who had a new baby, and we would play games like 'Kick the Can' or 'Gray Wolf.'"

"You didn't have chores, Mom," said Leonard, "so what did you do on Sunday afternoons?"

"Well," said Mom, "sometimes we would walk up to the neighbor's woods. First we had to cross a field, and so we would look carefully for any bulls and then duck under the fence. We would keep going until we reached the woods and came to the big tree that was covered with carved initials. Some of them were the initials of couples from long ago. We would try to figure out who all the couples were.

"When we would get home, Mom and Dad would just be getting up from an afternoon nap, and the boys would be hot and tired from bike riding. We would all poke our noses into the kitchen while Mom made supper. Often on Sunday evenings, she would make us bacon, lettuce, and tomato sandwiches. Then in the evenings we would go visiting or play games and eat popcorn."

"That was the life," Olive said. "You must wish you could be a little girl again."

"We did mission work there too," said Mom. "We would

visit older folks or neighbors whom we hardly knew. You can bless other people wherever you live. We children didn't like it when we visited older people and had to sit all evening with no toys, but it was good for us. And we had plenty of problems too. Sometimes we thought our parents weren't fair. Sometime we had spats with each other. We had the same struggles others have."

"I guess," Olive said reluctantly. She still thought life in Ohio sounded like a dreamy existence.

"I hear a car," Sandra piped up.

Suddenly Dad sat up straight and looked at Mom.

"I forgot to tell you that I invited Bob Julian and Doug Remington over tonight."

For a minute Mom was startled. "For supper?"

Dad nodded. "Sorry about that."

Mom relaxed again. "Well, I guess they can eat what we eat. I know neither one is particular about his food."

Dad answered the knock at the door. Olive flew around the kitchen, chopping avocados for Mom to make guacamole. Olive was glad avocados had been on sale when Mom went shopping, because that was something special to feed the men.

Bob did most of the talking, as usual. "I told Doug that I wish my wife were here to see the winter this year. She doesn't get to see much snow."

The children looked at him in surprise. "Don't they have snow in Israel?" asked Andrea.

"Only some years and in some places. My wife has to

stay home and work hard. She doesn't have time to travel. She's in the military, you know. And she teaches Arabic on the side."

Dad changed the subject, and Olive glanced at Doug. He was downing the food at a pretty high speed, and Olive wondered once again how much he had eaten through the week. He was able to work only part-time, and he had rent to pay. Some of the church families had discussed letting him live with one of them, but they had decided it would be best to wait until he became a Christian. How Olive hoped he would become a Christian soon!

Olive thought about the people they had seen on the streets that day, and a new thought hit her. Their group had offered the truth to anybody who was searching for it, but the next step in that work was happening right here in Frazier Park, at the Brennemans' house. It wouldn't do much good to pass out tracts if no one lived close by to invite people over for supper and show an interest in their lives. What if no one lived close enough to help them understand the Bible if they had questions?

Olive looked at Dad. He was busy listening to Bob. Olive didn't know of anyone who had more patience than Dad, and it was coming in handy right now. And she knew that Dad understood that mission work done at home is at the heart of what they were called to do. And, of course, he didn't want to miss the angels!

chapter seven

OLIVE'S EYES HAD HARDLY CLOSED WHEN she jerked awake. Vanderbilt was barking again. What was his problem? For the last week he had barked so much of the night, and Mom and Dad couldn't figure it out. They were tired of not getting a good night's sleep because Vanderbilt's doghouse was right outside their window.

"I guess we'll have to get rid of that dog," Mom had said. "I don't mind getting up a few times a night with babies, but I don't really feel like staying up because of that dog."

"It must be something," Dad had said with certainty. "Animals don't act like that unless there's something wrong. Maybe it's a mountain lion."

Olive shivered under her covers as she thought about mountain lions. Reportedly there were lots of them around. One had been killed on the road close to Frazier Park the week before, so there was proof.

The next morning after Dad went to work, he called Mom. Olive heard Mom's side of the conversation. "What? Really! It was that big? Did it kill the dog? What did Carlos say about that?"

"Must be a rattlesnake," concluded Leonard. "Something bit Carlos Hernández's dog." But when Mom got off the phone, she said it wasn't a rattlesnake.

"It was a mountain lion—a great big one, and it killed Carlos's dog. Carlos thought it was another dog or a coyote, and he threw a bottle of water at it. Then he saw it was a great big skinny mountain lion that was hungry enough to sneak into the housing development and attack the dog."

"Did it go back into the mountains?" Tabitha asked soberly, and Mom shook her head.

"No, it did not. Abram Miller's Troy came over and shot it."

Tabitha breathed an audible sigh. Olive sighed with relief too, only not out loud. Was she ever glad she didn't have to worry about meeting up with that animal!

"Do you think the game department will get Carlos or Troy into trouble since lions are protected?" Leonard wondered.

Mom shook her head again. "Carlos called them out right away this morning, and they hadn't moved the dog or the lion. Of course that was the right thing to do, and the game warden said it was fine, since it attacked his dog."

The next Monday night was the Brennemans' night to have the single men over for supper. The church ladies had decided to take turns inviting the men for supper one night a week. That way they would know the men were getting fed properly. They had typed up a schedule so everyone knew when their turn was. Olive liked the plan. She liked to listen to Bob Julian talk, and she liked Doug Remington with his gentle, nervous ways.

She liked when Carlos Hernández came too. He sometimes told stories about Cuba. He had grown up there with little to eat, and he had stayed in Cuba until he was middle-aged. When he had gotten a rare chance to come to the United States, he left his family behind. But now that he was a Christian, Carlos wished he could bring his wife to live with him. She wanted to come too, but it was taking a long time to persuade the Cuban government to let her go.

On this Monday night Carlos talked as much as Bob. He told them all about his mountain lion experience, and the Brenneman children were all ears. Then Dad asked him how the paperwork was coming for his wife, and Carlos talked a long time about Cuba.

"My wife will be amazed at your family," he said, looking around at the Brennemans. Olive looked at her family too. Was there something unusual about them?

"In Cuba everyone has one or two children," he explained. "And there are still not enough houses. No new houses have been built since 1975. So when a child gets married, the parents move upstairs, and the child's family lives downstairs."

"So we will be a gigantic family to her," Dad laughed.

"That's right. And she will be amazed at all this food and the size of your house."

"Leonard," Mom broke in, "take a basket and get the last of the towels off the line for me before it gets dark, please."

Leonard moseyed off to find a basket, and Olive went back to the book she was reading. Leonard had no more than gone out the door when he ran back in and slammed it behind him. "There's a bear out there!" he hollered. His eyes looked like dinner plates.

The whole Brenneman family and their visitors rushed out the front door to the deck as quietly as they could. There stood a black bear, strong and fearless, right below the clothes line, about two yards away from the towels still flapping in the breeze.

As soon as he saw the people, the bear started climbing the mountain. He stopped once or twice to look at them, and then he lumbered out of sight.

"Well," Mom exclaimed, a flabbergasted look on her face. "So that's why Vanderbilt has been throwing such a fit. And we were feeling upset at him for barking. Bless his canine heart for trying to warn us!"

Everybody started talking at once. Olive looked admiringly at Leonard. "You almost bumped into that bear."

"Aww, but I'm not very brave," Leonard said. "I couldn't help the bear was out there, could I? And did I get the towels and act like the bear was stuffed? No, I ran in just like any old baby would."

"Well, it's a good thing you did," Carlos told him. "You don't play around with wild animals, especially not one that big. We get this teddy bear concept sometimes . . ." he continued, launching into a mini-sermon about the danger of wild animals.

Bob had been unusually quiet, but now he began to talk. "I never saw a bear in Israel," he said, "although they used to live there. I'll have to tell my wife about this."

For the next few weeks, the little girls were traumatized by the bear episode and wouldn't play outside after supper anymore. Olive wouldn't have admitted it, but she didn't really enjoy going outside after supper herself. But as the weeks wore on and the bear kept stopping by almost every night, the whole family relaxed and got somewhat used to it. The bear seemed to show up for sure on Thursday evenings. That's when the Brennemans would set out their trash cans for the Friday morning trash pick-up, but the bear would push them over during the night, looking for something to eat.

"I declare," complained Mom. "We pay the trash company sixteen dollars a month to dispose of our trash, and now we can't even put our trash outside because of that bear!"

"You need to learn to cohabit with the bears," said Leonard sarcastically. "If you don't want to risk being eaten by bears, move out of the mountains." He said this because the local paper had been publishing lots of bear discussions the last while. It seemed as if there were multiple bears coming around, maybe because some of the big fires the year before had driven them to new territories. A lot of the locals were animal rights advocates, and they thought the bears were behaving themselves just fine. They said it was the people who were imposing on the bears.

"Well," Mom muttered as she went on with her work, "who was here first, I ask?" But that evening, when they saw the bear heading up the lane once more, even Mom had to admit that there was something fun about having a resident bear.

That night the girls went through what had become their normal bedtime ritual. "Mom!" yelled Tabitha and Andrea and Sandra. "We're scared! Can we sleep in your room?"

Dad went over the same lines he had gone over so many times lately. "How is the bear going to get into your room?"

"He can climb up the house."

"No, a bear wouldn't even try that."

"He can get a ladder."

"No, bears don't have ladders, and even if he wanted to borrow mine, they are safely locked in the basement."

"Well, maybe he'll knock down the door downstairs and sneak up the steps and eat us up."

"Girls." Dad's voice was firm. "Of course not. The door is locked. You just have to remember that God is in control. Try to think of something else and go to sleep."

"We might as well make a recording out of this and play it every night," laughed Olive, and Dad peered at her in the dim light.

"You were young once too," he reminded her.

Saturday night Mom put a pork roast in the crock pot for the Sunday fellowship meal. "There now," she said to her roast, "you just cook all night, and you'll be done perfectly in the morning." Dad had to preach in the morning, so all the Brennemans went to bed early. But they had slept only one hour when Vanderbilt started barking, making an awful racket.

Olive tossed and turned, but she just couldn't sleep through all that noise. Finally she got up and went down the stairs. Leonard was down there too! It was eleven o'clock when Dad finally traipsed down the steps with the spotlight. "Let's see what he's up to," he said. "We can't sleep anyway." He shone the spotlight over the hill, and the bear looked up guiltily at them from where he was licking a yogurt container from someone's trash can.

"Ha!" said Olive quietly. "That yogurt is probably old and moldy, and you have to work awfully hard for a few drops." They watched the bear for a while, and then they went back to bed and tried to sleep.

The dog kept on barking. At two o'clock Mom heard some thumping and bumping on the deck. *Is that the wind blowing something around on the deck?* she asked herself, *or is that the bear?* Finally she got up to check. She walked out and looked around. There he was, right at the bottom of the steps. He looked at Mom, and Mom looked at him. Suddenly it dawned on Mom why he was hanging around. "Why, it's that roast! I smell it myself!"

Mom picked up some little stones that were on the deck and threw them at him. "Now you go away," she said. "I said *get!*" Dad had joined her, and they watched as the bear tried to make up his mind. Finally he took off toward the gate that was blocking the path up the mountain. When he reached the gate, he crawled between the bars. He was moving pretty fast, but he had to put his one fuzzy back foot through the gate first and then lift the other one up behind him to put it through last. It looked so funny that Dad laughed out loud.

"I'm sorry that you can't get any sleep. How can you preach tomorrow morning?" Mom worried, but Dad didn't seem upset. "I will just trust God to give me an extra portion of His Spirit," he said, and went back to bed. Mom followed, but after another few hours of tossing and listening to the dog bark, she came down to the living room to sit on the recliner. Things were a little quieter in the living room, and just as she drifted off to sleep, something jiggled the side door.

Mom was wide awake in an instant. She jumped up and started toward the side door to tell the bear to go away, and then she thought better of it. What if the door didn't hold? She ran up the steps and met Dad headed down with his gun.

"I loaded my shotgun," he said. "I heard him knocking on the door."

Together they went to the door and watched as the bear finally took off up the mountainside. And at six o'clock in the morning, all was finally quiet.

Olive was sad to have missed some of the excitement. "I wish you had shot him," she said at breakfast. "Then we could have had bear jerky, like Mom is always talking about."

"You know, I was seriously thinking of shooting him," said Dad, "but then I thought about having a bear to butcher this morning when I have to preach. It just wouldn't have been very good timing."

Leonard didn't think that was an issue. "They could've had a song service since it would've been an emergency."

"Well," Dad finished, "it is Sunday, and we don't want to make work if we don't have to. Also I don't think the people who read the local paper would have been very happy with us, and maybe the California Department of Fish and Game wouldn't have been either. We want to remember to be a good testimony to the community. We are the only Bible some of them read."

Leonard nodded. "Yeah, I guess you're right. We'd better get a permit and do it right. But God told Adam and Eve to subdue the earth, and I think we have some subduing to do around here."

"But right now," said Dad, "you children had better stop talking and eat your breakfast, or we'll be late for church."

chapter eight

"WHAT'S THAT, JIM?" DAD ASKED. UNCLE Jim was sitting across the table after lunch on a Sunday afternoon.

Uncle Jim raised his voice so he could be heard above the general din. "I said I wonder if I couldn't get you a log house for the same price as a regular stick frame."

Dad shook his head. "I don't think you could. Of course, we love log homes, but I really don't want to spend more money than I have to."

"I can hardly believe we're building a house," Madeline said to Olive. "It's so exciting to think of it!"

"I know," Olive agreed. "Mom and Dad weren't even thinking of building a house right now, but land prices are going up. I heard Dad say more than once that he hoped he didn't have to raise a big family on a city lot like where we are now. So he got to thinking about building when he saw this big piece of land that's way cheaper than the land around it."

"Why is it cheaper?" asked Madeline.

"I don't know," Olive said. "Leonard, do you know?"

"A part of the land he's buying is on a fault line," Leonard informed them. "To build on that part of the land you would have to do a geo-dig."

The girls had no idea what a geo-dig was, but Leonard knew. That was his specialty, to learn the things Dad knew.

"A geo-dig," he began, "costs a lot of money. It's when you go through the proper procedures to dig a big hole so that you can see if the earth is firm enough to build where the fault line is. Otherwise, when an earthquake comes, you might just tumble into the cracks."

"So why aren't we scared that we might fall into the cracks?" Madeline wondered.

Leonard began to get a patient look on his face. "We won't build on that part of the land," he said. "Some people are worried they'll have to do a geo-dig and spend a lot of money only to find out they can't build where they want to. That's why they don't want to buy this land. Dad says we already know the fault line isn't close to where we want to build, so we won't have to do a geo-dig."

"Anyway," Olive said, "won't it be fun to have acres and acres of land to roam?"

"Not to burst your bubble," Leonard said, "but it's almost all mountainside."

Olive nodded. "I knew that, but we can still take walks

up the mountain. That's better than two small city lots, like where we are now."

Uncle Jim was nodding. "Yes, I think now's your time. You just give me those house plans. I'm going to send them to my old boss in Ohio to see what he can do."

Dad meekly handed the plans over to Uncle Jim for him to study. "I don't think it would be hard," Uncle Jim said. "It's just a rectangle with three stories."

"That's what we want," agreed Dad, "just a plain old house. But my, wouldn't we love a log house! Better not get our hopes up, though," he added. "Logs are expensive, and we can't pay much more just to have a log house."

It was two weeks until Uncle Jim got back to them, and what he had to say was exciting! His boss thought a log house could be built in California for about the same price as a regular house, since the cost of a regular wood-frame house was more in California than it was in Ohio, and a log house would cost the same at both places.

Olive thought she couldn't wait another two months till the permits came through and the plans were approved. "What do you think?" she heard Dad asking Mom. "Should we go ahead and sell the house and live somewhere temporarily until the new one is built? We really need the money right now."

Mom was happy with that plan. She worried that they really couldn't afford a new house. "I never dreamed about getting a new house," she said. "It makes me feel like we're doing something that only rich people do."

"I know what you mean," Dad said. "But doesn't it seem like God has answered our prayers for more space for the family? I mean, it's amazing that the land we were wanting has waited a year on us, with everything selling like hotcakes around it!"

Mom had to agree.

"Why are we going to sell the house?" Sandra asked in a worried voice. Dad picked her up and threw her into the air.

"Now don't you worry your head about it. We'll make sure you have a place to sleep and . . ." Dad put Sandra down and tweaked one of her braids, "five sisters for you to play with." Sandra laughed and ran off to find her favorite doll.

"Where *are* we going to live?" Olive asked Dad. "Are we going to rent a house or a camper or something?"

"I like the camper idea," said Mom. "Can't we get a big one and sell it again?"

Dad was pretty skeptical. "I don't know," he said. "We'd have to get a pretty big travel trailer for this family, and what if all the plumbing breaks when I'm trying to build a new house? I won't have time for that."

"That's true," Mom said, "but what if none of the plumbing breaks, and we have lots of fun building the house as a family? I hate to miss out if you're going to be there every day. You never worked at home since we were married. But if you think it's not practical, then . . ."

Dad stroked his beard for a long time. "Those campers

are always breaking," he muttered, "but if we could find a newer model and I could sell it when we're done with it, then maybe."

A few weeks later, Grandma and Grandpa Birky came to visit, so one day the whole family took a little vacation and went north to see the Sequoia trees. On the way home they drove through a little town, and what did they see for sale along the road but a nice long travel trailer?

"Shall we stop?" Dad asked, and the whole family chorused a "yes." Dad called the number on the sign, and the lady came right over. She unlocked the travel trailer and showed Mom and Dad inside.

"Do you think we'll get it?" Olive asked Leonard.

Leonard shook his head. "You know Dad never does things fast like that."

"I hope we do," said Madeline. "Wouldn't that be fun to live in there?"

"Where would we all sleep?" Tabitha wondered. "Maybe we'll have to make beds on the roof."

Grandma laughed. "I don't think that would be very practical. It would be better to sleep on the kitchen table than on the roof."

Mom and Dad came back to the van, and as they drove home, they discussed the trailer. "The lady said she hadn't wanted to sell it," said Mom, "but her husband was the one who took care of it, and now he has Alzheimer's. So maybe she'll give us a good deal if she's not really trying to make money."

"Where would we sleep?" Tabitha wondered again.

"Well," said Dad, "there's a nice bedroom in the one end with a double bed, and then there's the full sized sofa with a hide-a-bed . . ."

"I think it would be fun," Olive said, "like living in another country or something."

Dad turned around and looked at the excited children. "The fun may last only so long," he said. "But hopefully it will be only a few months after we move out of the old house till we get into the new one."

The next week Dad called the lady and told her they would take the trailer. The real estate agent stopped by to look at the old house and talked to Dad and Mom about a fair price to ask for it. Soon it was listed in the paper.

"This is more work than I realized," said Olive. "We have to keep our house in such good order all the time because we never know who might be stopping by to look at it."

"Olive, you shouldn't complain," Madeline reminded her. "The sooner we sell our house, the sooner we can move to the trailer."

"I know," Olive sighed. "But I get tired of being patient. And the logs are coming next week."

Olive thought about the last few weeks and how exciting it had been to see the dirt packed and the basement poured for the new house. It almost seemed like a dream. And to think that they would get to live on that nice private land! Now, to top it off, Uncle Joshua and Uncle Merle and their families were planning to come for a few weeks, and they were all going to help with the new house.

Olive was glad her relatives were carpenters. Uncle Merle had a daughter who was just her age, and Olive was looking forward to being together. It wasn't often that she got to be with her cousins from back East. What a family reunion it would be! Olive felt warm feelings toward her uncles when she thought about how they were paying all that money to bring their families to California to help with the building project.

* * * *

Building the house was kind of like building with Lincoln Logs. Olive and her cousin Emily watched Uncle Merle and Uncle Joshua lay another log on the walls with the help of a machine. Then they glued it and screwed it down with great big screws, and it was as sturdy as if it had grown that way. Uncle Jim was busy with a chainsaw, getting the next log ready to put up.

The girls walked inside the walls. It was so cheerful with the sun streaming in the holes cut for windows. Little chips of wood and nails lay all over the floor. It still took some imagination to think of it being a finished house.

Leonard and Uncle Merle's son Ed, who was a year older than Leonard, ambled over to the girls.

"Do you think we ruined the habitat for any California condors?" Leonard asked, looking at Olive.

"What are condors?" Emily wanted to know.

"They're the biggest land birds in the United States," Olive told her. "Don't you study about them in school in Ohio?"

Emily shook her head. "I don't think so, but well, I don't like science, so if I did, I might have forgotten it."

"I agree with you about science," Olive said. "Leonard, tell Emily about condors."

It didn't take Leonard long to warm up to a subject like that. "California condors are scavengers," he began. "The big thing about condors is that they're endangered, which means that they're almost extinct. In 1987 there were only twenty-two California condors left, and they were all in captivity."

"Wow," said Ed, duly impressed. "Are there any more now?"

"There are," Leonard informed him. "I just checked it out lately, and they say there are 405 now, with over two hundred in the wild."

"Why does it matter?" Emily asked. "I mean, what would change on our earth if there were no more condors?"

Leonard shook his head. "I don't really know, except that all organisms are needed to keep the cycle of nature in balance. Something needs to eat the dead animals."

"Yuck," said Olive. "I certainly don't care enough to write in the paper about it like some people here do."

"Do you know," Leonard asked, looking at Ed and Emily, "that some people were trying to put in a wind farm a few miles from here?"

"What is a wind farm?" Emily asked.

"A farm that somebody talks about but that doesn't exist?" Ed joked.

Olive laughed as loud as she wanted since they were in the great outdoors. It was so fun to have cousins around!

"Actually, it's just a place where they make electricity with a bunch of windmills," Leonard explained. "There's one about an hour's drive from here. But what does it have to do with condors? Well, the people near here fought the idea of a wind farm here because the condors fly through these mountains. They were afraid the condors would be killed in the windmills."

"And they got the wind farm stopped," added Olive. "But I don't care either way about the condors. They're actually pretty ugly."

The boys walked away, and the girls watched the men again.

"Do you think you'll sell your other house soon?" Emily asked Olive.

"We had five people through to look at it last week," she said. "Dad thinks it will sell soon, but he says it's fine if we don't have to move out yet, or we'll get tired of the trailer."

Summer was almost over when the papers were finally signed on the old house. The Ohio relatives had all gone home, but Grandpa Birky was going to make another trip out to bring the kitchen cabinets he was building for the house. This time he was bringing Grandma and Uncle Conrad with him.

The Brennemans were very busy getting ready to move and getting the trailer ready. Dad had hauled a few truckloads of sand to the place where the trailer would sit.

At first Olive wasn't too sure about sand all over the place, but when she saw how sticky and black the soil was, she was glad she had a wise dad.

"How did we ever get so much stuff?" sighed Mom on moving day as the church men hauled the last few boxes out to the old box truck Dad had bought to haul and store their things. "How thankful I am for the people from church!"

They were at the trailer working when Olive heard a voice behind her. "Doesn't look like there's much left for me to do."

"Oh, Aunt Marge," Olive exclaimed, "I didn't know you were here!"

"I'm late. Can I help you do something in the trailer?"

Mom smiled a tired smile. "You can help us unpack the few boxes that go into the trailer, but you know how travel trailers are. They come with curtains and all, and there's not that much to do."

It was amazing how much there *was* to do, though, as the Brenneman family set up housekeeping in the camper. It really felt like they were camping. Dad put the washer and dryer outside, and even the big refrigerator was out there. Mom had used the small refrigerator inside for storage space.

Abram Miller offered to loan them his smaller trailer for some extra bedroom space, but he warned them that there was a leak in the roof. Dad took him up on the offer, although he wasn't quite sure what to do about the leak. But since it usually doesn't rain in the summer and early fall in California, he had some time to think about what to do. He had rented a little temporary bathroom to put outside, because with eight children, one bathroom would hardly be enough.

That evening the Brenneman family stood outside their camper trailer and surveyed their little home. Dad had parked the two trailers in an L shape. He had put the swing set in the sand in front of them, and close by was the temporary bathroom. If they looked up the hill, they could see the new house with the bright logs. It was a nice little camp, and Olive thought it was an interesting way to live.

The fun wore off, though, as the days went by. The house was taking much longer to build than Dad had thought. At first it was fun to sleep with three on the couch bed, two on the floor, and two in the other trailer, but after a while it got old. It was a hassle to fold all the bedding every morning, and since winter was nearing, the little trailer got cold. Mom tried to be cheerful about it.

"Just think of the memories you're making," she said to Olive and Madeline as they headed out to the smaller trailer with their lantern. "What other girl in California gets to use a lantern at night time?"

"It's kind of cozy," Madeline admitted to Olive as they snuggled under their covers. But by morning it was not cozy. They'd had the first rain of the season, and the leak in the roof was right above their bed. Dad knew something would have to be done, so after a trip to the hardware store, he stretched a blue tarp over the top.

"Now we really look like hillbillies," Mom laughed as she looked out the window at the blue-tarped roof.

When Dad came in for supper, he told Mom, "You'd better look at your schoolroom over in the other trailer. I found another leak in the kitchen."

"Oh, no," Mom said. "Leonard and Olive, you go see what it looks like."

They checked out the school things. It had been working out well to have Aunt Marge watch the younger children while Mom took the older ones over to the trailer to have school. But now they looked in dismay as they realized that some of the charts and books were wet. Leonard figured out where the water was coming in, and Olive moved everything to a safe place. There were just some things that weren't going to be perfect this school year.

* * * *

Doug Remington and Bob Julian had been coming for supper on Monday nights before the Brennemans moved to the trailer, and Dad didn't see any reason why they had to stop now. It was a little tough to set the table for extra people, but they managed.

One Monday evening when Doug came, Mom sat in the kitchen to eat so that there would be enough room at the table. Doug, being soft-hearted, could hardly stand to see Mom sitting in the kitchen, but Mom insisted. "Just relax," she told him. "I'm not suffering."

Olive watched Doug when they had family devotions. He sat very respectfully and even helped some with the singing.

He was slowly learning the songs from church. Olive again wondered about his past life. Doug had told someone that he had two sons who were grown up. Olive thought about how awful it would be to be homeless and know that your family didn't care enough to take you in.

After supper Doug talked to Dad for a long time. Dad told them the next morning that Doug was really emotionally upset because his health was bad, and he knew that he must stop abusing his body or he was headed for an early death. Dad talked to the other brothers from church, and they decided to encourage Doug to get help at a place in the city that helped folks like him get off drugs. The Brennemans prayed that Doug would be willing. Maybe then he would be ready to give his life to God.

Several days later a family who lived three hours north of Frazier Park called. They were friends of the Brennemans, and they wondered if they could stop in to visit.

"Plan to have supper with us," Mom offered, but as she said it, she knew it would be hard to fit them in. It was too cold to sit outside. The caller accepted the invitation, leaving Mom wondering what she had just done.

While Aunt Marge got the wash going, Mom got the school children busy and began making food. Because the kitchen was small, everything was at her fingertips. But the lack of floor space was a problem. And the dirt! With so many people in such a small living area, dirt accumulated quickly.

"I don't know what I would be doing without you,

Marge," Mom said as she surveyed the clouds in the sky. "Do you think the laundry will dry?"

"I doubt it," answered Aunt Marge. "This is not a good drying day."

"We've got company coming," worried Mom. "Maybe you'd better go to the Laundromat."

Aunt Marge was thrilled to do that. She got so frustrated with doing laundry in uncooperative weather. While she loaded up, Mom went to the schoolroom and helped the older children.

"Look who's coming," Leonard said, peeking out the little trailer window.

"Leonard, keep working," Mom told him for the third time that morning.

"But it's the man who cleans the outside bathroom."

"All right, you may look a little," Mom relented, and the children opened the trailer door to get a better look. The big round man who cleaned the bathroom was becoming a friend. They had such fun watching him do his job. He had a resigned look that seemed to say that if this was what he had to do, he might as well do it well.

The bathroom man was hosing out the bathroom when suddenly Olive said, "Look!"

The man had a roll of toilet paper under his arm, and some of the paper had unrolled and was flapping in the wind as he hosed. It made a funny picture, to be sure, but Mom said they needed to get back to their school work. She shut the trailer door as they all doubled up laughing.

When the company came that evening, the Brennemans lined up chairs in the living room, just as the children did when they played train, and everyone had enough space to sit and eat supper. It worked just fine, and afterward the children played outside beneath the light Dad had put up.

"Where there's a will, there's a way," said Mom, "but I'm getting anxious to have a normal house again."

There was progress at the new house, but it was slow. Finally the windows were in place and the few walls that were not going to have exposed logs were ready for drywall and painting. Mom spent as much time as she could working with Dad in the new house, and she even moved the washer and dryer to the new basement. It was a lot of work to haul all the laundry up the hill, but it was cheaper than the Laundromat. The little trailer was cold, so Mom moved the school things up to the new kitchen. For a while it was fun to do schoolwork while the drywall man and the plumber and the trim carpenter worked around them.

"I wonder what they think of us doing our schoolwork," Olive said to Dad one day after Mom had drilled one of the children for a social studies quiz. "They hear what we believe sometimes."

"That's fine," said Dad. "It's a unique way to witness. But I do think our drywall man takes something that alters his mind sometimes. I'm getting frustrated at how little he works."

"I agree," Mom said from the bathroom where she was painting. She was frustrated with the drywall man too, but what could they do now that they had already hired him? "I think we hired too many down-and-outers," she added, "but I guess, like you said, it's a way of witnessing."

"I think it's time to return to more traditional ways of witnessing," said Dad. "I'm ready to move in."

By the time the Brennemans moved into their new house, they were good and tired of camping. Living in the new house felt like living in a mansion, even if some of the trim wasn't finished and the outside logs still needed to be coated with a protective coating. It was a good solid house, and Dad was happy. So was Uncle Jim. "It gives me some satisfaction to know that I really can build a log home with a little direction from my old boss," he said.

Olive thought back over the process of building the house and all the ways people had helped them. She remembered the funny songs Uncle Jim sang to entertain them as he worked and the way he sat on the floor sander to make it work better while Dad sanded. She thought of the uncles who flew in from back East to help and all the church ladies who helped with meals. She thought about Aunt Marge who had come every day to do whatever needed to be done. So many people had helped make their house a reality, and she knew it was a very special house.

chapter nine

"IT'S SNOWING. IT'S SNOWING!" TABITHA and Andrea shouted as they looked out the window one cold winter day. The Brennemans all flew to the window as Mom frowned.

"Children, come back to the table and do your schoolwork. You've seen snow before."

"But not this year," Olive said.

Mom smiled. "I'm ready for snow myself. I hope we get a bunch. But please finish your schoolwork now."

The children reluctantly got back to work. But their eyes kept wandering to the windows, watching the big snowflakes pour down.

"Do you hear that wind?" Leonard asked. "I think this is going to be a big one."

Tabitha shivered. She hated wind. Whenever there were high winds, she was scared to go to sleep. What if the house tumbled down? Mom and Dad had assured her over and over that the house was strong and a little wind wouldn't hurt it, but her fear was still there. The shrieking of the wind did make the log house seem cozy, and Mom even made some tea for a treat.

Olive tried to keep her mind on her work. It seemed so elegant to drink tea while doing school assignments, but she just wanted to get done so that she could watch it snow.

It was afternoon when Grandma Brenneman called. Olive heard Mom talking. "Yes, it's snowing—has been since this morning. Oh, I don't know how much it is, but it's really piling up."

"Let's measure it," Leonard suggested, so they took the ruler out to the back yard.

"Ten inches," he said as he shut the door quickly. It was exciting to have so much snow and not know when it was going to stop.

"How's Dad going to get home?" wondered Andrea.

Mom looked up from her cooking. "Oh, he'll probably just get up the road part way, and then he'll have to walk. But come to think of it, I hope they let him up the freeway."

"Do you think the freeway is closed?" Olive asked, and Mom nodded.

"It's sure to be, unless there is no snow down there. Maybe I should call Aunt Judy to see if they have any." Uncle Craig and Aunt Judy lived about 1,500 feet lower than the Brennemans and closer to the elevation of the freeway. Sometimes they didn't get snow when the Brennemans did.

But Aunt Judy said they did have snow. They had the same amount. "So the freeway will be closed," Mom concluded. "I hope they let Dad through. He does have a four-wheel-drive pickup."

At about five o'clock, Dad called. "I got through," he said. "I had to show my license, but they said to go ahead. It feels funny to drive on an empty freeway."

It was six o'clock when Dad thumped up the steps to the house. He looked like a snowman, and he hadn't really dressed for the weather, since he was working in the warm valley. But here he was, and it made Olive feel better to know that the family was all home. Let the winds and the snow blow now!

The next morning the snow was still falling. Grandma Brenneman called again. "Yes," Mom told her, "it is still falling. Leonard measured it this morning, and we have twenty-four inches."

After Mom hung up, she said, "Grandma is surprised we have so much snow. I guess when people think of southern California, they just don't think of snow. They think only of oranges."

"It's different than the snow we got back East," Dad said over the paper he was reading. "It's so much colder there. Really, we get the best of both worlds. It isn't so cold, and yet it's just cold enough to snow."

"And it starts melting right away," added Mom. "I'm trying not to think of the big muddy mess when this is over."

"Aww, don't ruin the fun," Leonard said. "Why don't we get our work done early and play Monopoly tonight?"

In the morning it had stopped snowing, so Dad started working. First he shoveled off the roof. Three feet of snow was hard on it, he said. Then he went to see how the neighbors were faring. Meanwhile the children bundled up to go out and play. Just before they went out the door, Madeline began to laugh. "Look," she said. "Look at Vanderbilt!"

They all looked out the side window, and even Zachary had to giggle. The snow was level with the window, and Vanderbilt was walking on top of it. He was at the end of his rope, looking straight in at them. The children decided to build their snowman by his doghouse to keep him company.

When Mom looked up a while later, she saw a snowman so big that the children were using a ladder to put his head on. Then the children began trailing through the house for carrots and a hat and mittens for the snowman. Mom hoped they'd come in soon so that she could clean up the mess.

When they all came in, cold and rosy, they couldn't stop talking about the fun. "I pity the folks who don't have snow," said Olive. "Only they probably don't know what they're missing."

"About half of Los Angeles will try to find out what they're missing," Leonard said. "Wait till tomorrow when everyone's off work."

Mom turned from wiping up the floor. "Dad said he saw the TV reporters doing their job, so people will know there is snow up here. We haven't had this much snow at one time for several years, so I'm sure it will attract the tourists."

Dad burst in the door, looking weary from fighting the snow. "The neighbors were out shoveling," he explained, "and so I helped them a while. But it's really kind of fruitless. We need a skid loader. I wish I had one."

"Abram Miller will plow us out eventually, won't he?" asked Mom hopefully.

"I imagine he will, but right now we'd better work on clearing a path down to the bottom of the lane so that we can at least walk up and down a little easier. Come on, Leonard, let's see how strong your biceps are."

"I want to go too," Olive pleaded. "Don't you think I have strong biceps?"

Dad sized up Olive. "Why not?" he said. "We can use all the help we can get."

"I'd like to shovel some myself," Mom said. "I'll be the first to admit that my arms are pretty weak, but I'd like some fresh air."

"Sure," Dad answered as he walked out the door, but he didn't seem to think it would happen. It did, though. When the little ones were sleeping in the afternoon, Mom donned a coat and Dad's old work boots and went out to shovel. Dad had gone over to help the neighbors some more, and he was surprised to see Mom hard at work when he came back.

"I'm having fun," Mom told him. "It's like working in a postcard out here, with the snow hanging on the trees and all. Did you get any of the neighbors dug out yet?"

"We got Samantha out, neighbor Tom and I. She was ever so grateful because her mom needed to go to the doctor."

"Bless Tom's heart," said Mom. "He doesn't just talk about serving God; he puts it into practice."

"If there ever was a man who seems to have a humble heart, it's Tom," Dad agreed. "There he is, at age sixty, shoveling snow from the neighbor's lane for all he's worth."

It took a few days for the snow to melt enough for good sledding. Then Mom had more messes to deal with. She sighed as the children put on layers of tights and socks and madly scrambled through the glove drawer to find gloves that matched. One afternoon the children went sledding. They were gone for several hours, and Mom was beginning to worry about them. Finally they stomped up the steps and burst in the door, flinging bits of snow all over the place.

"We went sledding with Grandma Kay!" Olive exclaimed, the first to catch her breath.

"Grandma Kay?" Mom was surprised. The neighbor lady they called Grandma Kay was in her seventies, so it was hard to imagine her sledding.

"After we finished sledding," Madeline said, "she told us to come in for hot chocolate."

"And it had marshmallows in it," added Tabitha.

"To think," said Leonard, "that they're picking oranges in the valley."

"Yes, California is the home for hard-to-please people," Mom said. "If you don't like the weather in one place, either wait three days or drive for half an hour. And speaking of drives—I need groceries badly. What am I going to do?"

Dad thought maybe they should just get some things at the local market, but Mom wasn't sure. "You know we'll spend a lot more money up here, and I *really* need a lot of groceries."

"Well," said Dad, "I don't care if you go to Bakersfield, but how in the world will we get the groceries up here to the house?"

Mom thought for a little, and then she brightened up. "Couldn't we pull them up on the sled?"

Dad raised his one eyebrow. "It's hard enough to walk up through all that snow, let alone pull a sled loaded with groceries."

"Surely we can do it, little by little," Mom said. "But if you really don't think I should . . ."

"Go ahead," said Dad. "Only keep it in mind, and don't get enough for three months or anything."

Mom took the car, and Olive and Zachary went along. Mom needed someone to help her with the groceries.

"Whew, this is the first time I'll have been away since the snow," Mom said as they squished their way down the muddy path. The snow was wetter and heavier than when it had fallen, and it had already sunk to a foot and a half in just a few days.

The car was parked at the end of the lane, but it still had

deep snow on it. Helpful Tom was out shoveling, and he came over and tried to help Mom get it off, but the snow was covered with ice and was stuck fast.

"I'll just have to let it come off as I drive, but thanks anyway," Mom told Tom, but Tom shook his head.

"That might hurt someone," he warned.

"Oh, I didn't think about that," agreed Mom. "I guess if I was going fast, it might hit a car behind me. What shall we do?"

"I'll get a bucket of hot water, and you turn the heat on in the car," said Tom, disappearing down the road toward his house. It was only a few minutes until the big chunks of icy snow lay beside the car, and Mom, Olive, and Zachary started off.

As they rounded the corner into Frazier Park, Mom's mouth dropped open. "What is going on, anyway?"

The town park was jam-packed with cars, as was the post office parking lot and every other available space. A policeman was at the four-way stop directing the traffic. As Mom and Olive drove down the mountain, the cars came toward them in an almost solid line. People were trying to get to the snow.

"I'm glad we're going this way," Olive said. "Let's hope the crowds are gone by the time we come back."

It wasn't long until Mom and Olive and Zachary were on the freeway driving away from the snow. The trip to town was as normal as could be.

"I wonder how Doug Remington is doing," Mom said

after they had finished shopping and were headed home through the streets of Bakersfield.

"I wonder too," said Olive. "He sure seemed to want help."

"He's an example of humility for us," Mom added thoughtfully. "We sure don't want to start thinking we are perfect and can't take lessons from someone less fortunate. I really think that man is close to the kingdom of God."

"I guess it's good we're here then," said Olive, and Mom smiled at her.

"That's right, Olive. Seeing someone come to the Lord is so rewarding! Someday I hope you'll understand by experience how much more rewarding it is to serve God where He's called you than it is to live in the perfect climate. That reminds me—I should stop and see how Rosie Saldaña is getting along."

"Do we have time?" Olive wondered.

Mom glanced at her watch. "I think we do. We'd better stop while we can, because who knows how long it will be until we get down here again." Rosie lived just a few miles off the highway in Bakersfield, and they had known her for quite a while. The thing that was special about her was that her son lived in Pennsylvania and went to a church that was similar to the Brennemans' church. For his sake they tried to visit her now and then. Olive really didn't like going to nursing homes to sing for the elderly people, but Rosie was different. She was spunky for an eighty-year-old lady. She was originally from Mexico, and her parents had been migrant workers.

The first sound they heard when they knocked was the dog. The dog always threw a fit when they came.

"Shut up, will you?" Rosie scolded as she opened the door. Then she looked up, smiling. "Come in, come in. Oh, shut up," she scolded again. "That dog! He never will listen."

Mom smiled too. This was a normal way to be greeted at Rosie's house. "How are you doing, Rosie?" she asked.

"Oh, I'm fine. My eyes are bad, though. The doctor wants me to have surgery, but my blood pressure's too high. Sit down a while."

"Well," said Mom, "are you watching your diet?"

"He didn't tell me to. I'm taking pills, though. I take so many pills a day that I'm not hungry."

"Why would that make you not hungry?" Olive asked. Rosie whirled around to look at her.

"It's all that water I drink," she said. "I have to wash them down with something."

Mom and Olive laughed, but Rosie jumped on to another subject. "Do you folks need meat? I have some chicken here, but I can't eat it. I have only one tooth."

Rosie didn't have to tell them that. Olive had seen it the minute they walked in. It was a front tooth, and it hung there as if it wanted to drop out and join the rest.

"Sure, we can always use chicken," Mom agreed. "Maybe we can bring you some fruit in exchange."

"That would be fine. But I can't eat hard fruit, you know. Oh, dog, will you stop barking? I know you don't like to be penned up in the other room, but you're too loud." Rosie trotted off to deal with her dog, and Mom and Olive got up to go.

"Let me get that chicken," Rosie said, and in no time at all they were on the road again.

It didn't seem long until they rose up out of the warm valley and headed toward the mountains. It was almost a shock to come back up to all the muddy, snowy mess. It was dark already when Mom pulled into the parking spot at the end of the driveway.

"Now for the climb to the house," she said, and Olive groaned.

"You take Zachary," Mom directed. "I'll load the sled."

Mom took out the things that needed to go into the freezer and the things that she needed right away. "Oh, dear," she said, "Vanderbilt needs his dog food tonight. Leonard had to use cat food this morning. I really don't want to lug that big bag up the hill, though." She thought for a minute and then took an extra grocery bag and put a little dog food into it.

"There now," she said, "we're ready to go." Zachary was crying because he had been sleeping, and a cold walk wasn't a very nice way to wake up. Mom gripped the sled and began to walk. It took quite a while to get up the path, with Mom stopping to rest, but they finally got there. Dad came out to carry the groceries up the steps.

"Mrs. Determined got back okay," he teased Mom, but Mom just sat on the recliner to catch her breath.

"I'm glad I went," she said. "And who cares if the rest of the groceries stay in the car-pantry for a few days. At least we have supplies now."

"They're calling for snow next week again," Leonard put in, and Mom rolled her eyes.

"Snow is exciting, but I would be happy if it came as rain."

"You told us that God knows what to send, so we shouldn't complain," said Andrea.

"You're right," Mom agreed. "And besides," she added, "more snow would certainly give us something to write home about!"

chapter ten

BOB JULIAN WAS GONE, AND THE MEN who stood around the smoky grill at the Tejon Park were discussing it. Olive sat on the picnic table and listened to them. Why had Bob left?

"He asked me some strange questions before he left," Dad said. "The last time we had him over for supper, he asked me if we ever went fishing on Lake Erie when we lived in Ohio."

"Why did he want to know that?" preacher Abram wondered, raising his eyebrows in the way he always did when he was puzzled.

"That wasn't all he asked me," Dad continued. "He wondered if we were able to go to any of the little islands off the shore of Lake Erie. And then he wondered if we could take a fishing boat to any of the Canadian islands without going through customs."

"Not that he wanted to do that," added one of the church brothers, and all the men laughed.

"That's just it," Dad said. "Bob claimed he wanted to take his dad there for a vacation, and he was just curious."

The men shook their heads.

"Olive, why don't you come play pitch and catch with me?" said a voice beside her, and Olive moved over to let her friend Shannon Herr sit beside her. Shannon was a new friend—she had just moved in two months before, from farther south in California. Before that, her family had lived in South Africa.

When Olive first met the Herr family, she was surprised to see that they were blond and blue-eyed. Olive thought everyone from Africa was dark-skinned. But Shannon's mother assured her, in her soft British-sounding accent, that many Europeans had emigrated to South Africa years before, and their descendants were still living there.

Olive loved the way the Herr family spoke, though sometimes it confused her. Shannon had said her older brother wanted to be a "pasta." What first came to Olive's mind was macaroni and spaghetti, and then she realized that Shannon meant "pastor."

Shannon was waiting patiently for Olive to reply. Did Olive want to play with her or not?

"It's interesting to hear the men talk, but I guess I'll come," Olive finally answered and jumped up. "But first I want to show you something."

"What is it?" Shannon asked, following her to a large oak

tree near the edge of the park.

"It's a grave," Olive said solemnly. "Look."

Shannon shivered. "What does it say on that tree?"

"It's a plaque explaining who is buried here. Read it."

Shannon read slowly. "Oh, it says this tree used to have a message carved on it—it said 'Peter Lebec, killed by an X bear 1837.' What is an X bear, Olive?"

"Sometimes the old-timers called grizzly bears X bears. We don't have grizzly bears anymore, but the historians think they must have lived here at one time."

"Oooh," Shannon shivered again. "Why did you bring me over here to show me something so ghastly?"

"I wanted you to know more about the history of this part of California since you live here now. The reason this village is called Lebec is because of that man who was killed by a bear. Doesn't that make you feel more at home than you did a few minutes ago?" Olive asked, smiling at her friend.

Shannon laughed, "South Africa still feels like home to me. Somehow I don't think knowing that Lebec is named after a poor man killed by a grizzly bear will change that very much."

"Did you know that camels used to be here too?" Olive wondered.

Shannon looked at Olive incredulously. "Camels in California?"

"Yeah, Leonard told me all about it. He got a book at the library once, and I read about it later in our California history book. They brought them over here as an experiment, to see if camels were suited to this climate."

"Did it work?" Shannon wondered.

"Not really," Olive said. "Actually, the camels did a lot of things well, but nobody really knew much about handling them, and they ate a lot of food. The government decided they weren't worth their feed, and soon after they came, they were sent to another town to be auctioned off."

Shannon and Olive joined in the games. As Olive sat on the ground and waited her turn for a glove, her eyes wandered over the grounds of Tejon Park. What would this place have been like when it really was a fort? Olive had this secret desire to watch the war re-enactment that the community sometimes put on at this fort, but she knew she would never be allowed. Leonard had asked to go one time, and Dad had explained that it would be a poor testimony to the community for their family to show up at a war re-enactment when they had worked for years to teach what nonresistance meant. Besides that, he had said, it would be wrong for the Brenneman family to take part in the patriotism that normally accompanied a re-enactment like that.

"What is patriotism?" wondered Tabitha, and Dad went on to explain that watching the war re-enactments made you feel as if you were in the battle, and of course you would rejoice when the side you hoped would win, won. You would feel pride in the American soldiers who were brave and fought until death. And there would be rejoicing in the death of the enemy. And that was exactly the opposite of what Jesus taught when He told people to love their enemies and do good to the people who hated them.

Olive had agreed in her heart, but part of her still wished she could see it. The Brenneman family *had* come one day when the Fort Tejon buildings were unlocked for folks to look inside, and it had been really interesting to see pictures of the captain who led the fort. Fort Tejon had been built more than one hundred fifty years before when a lot of Indians still lived in California. It had been designed to help protect both white people and Indians from attacks by the more aggressive Indians. Olive had studied this in her California history book.

"Your turn," said Shannon, plopping down beside Olive and handing her a glove. Olive jumped up to play pitch and catch, but her mind still wandered to the things of the past. She had imagined life at the fort until she almost felt like she was a part of it. She was standing on the same land that those people had walked. That captain had been real, and all the soldiers had been real too.

The song called "What Will You Do With Jesus" kept running through Olive's head. Those people at the fort had done something with Jesus, long, long ago. Olive knew that she was coming to a crossroads in her own life. She had often heard Dad and Mom speak of the day when God would call their children to come to Him, and Olive wanted to obey when that time came for her. She didn't really feel called yet, but she felt serious about life. She felt like she was beginning to understand the difference knowing God made in someone's life.

"It's time to go," Dad called to the children, and Olive gathered up the ball gloves. Leonard looked hot and dusty as he walked beside her to the van.

"Dad said we're having a special meeting at church tomorrow afternoon," he told her.

"Why?"

"Because Eli Glick is coming to visit, and he's going to talk about El Salvador."

Olive was surprised. "You mean the Eli Glick who was kidnapped and someone wrote a book about?"

"I think."

"That will be interesting!" Olive loved missionary stories. She hoped to be a missionary herself someday, and she really loved reading stories of thrilling missionary escapes. She admired the people who were brave enough to live under dangerous circumstances. And now Eli could see how Miguel Juarez, the boy who had run away from his church and now repented, was doing. They had just taken Miguel in as a church member in the spring, and the church enjoyed his ever-present smile. That's how Miguel communicated best—but he was learning English fast.

Olive felt lazy when she got home. The Brenneman family all sat in the living room and wondered why school picnics made you feel that way. Finally Mom got up and made some supper, but nobody was very hungry.

When Sunday afternoon arrived, Olive waited expectantly for Eli Glick to begin speaking. He looked like a regular man—a very thin regular man—but Olive found it fascinating to see someone she had read about. A lot of what he said about El Salvador was in the book, but it was different to hear it from the lips of the man who had experienced it. Eli talked about some things that were hard for him to understand about the experience. Olive was surprised at that. It seemed that a man as old and wise as Eli would understand everything about God.

Olive glanced at Miguel. He seemed happy to see his old friend again, and Olive was so glad Miguel was there to make Eli glad.

Olive thought about the things she struggled with in California. Why, nothing seemed like a hardship after hearing about Eli's kidnapping! Olive thought that after being kidnapped, regular life would seem like a piece of cake, but Eli seemed to think life was still a battle.

"Are you getting used to American ways yet?" Olive asked Shannon as they sat on the front porch of the mission house after church.

"I guess we are. You know we've been in California for two years now."

Olive could tell Shannon really did miss her homeland, and she loved to listen to Shannon talk. "So how is it different here?" Olive asked her.

"Well, in South Africa we had servants," Shannon began. "They were black servants, but we paid them, of course. Mom loves to cook, so she would make our meals, but then when we were done, we called out the back door to Betty, and Betty would clean up."

"Wow!" Olive exclaimed. "Wow! Now that would be great!"

"Maybe," said Shannon, "but it causes a lot of problems between people of different colors. And it affects the way we think too. We didn't realize how much it affected us until we left South Africa. When we flew to the United States, we first landed in the Netherlands. My mother was amazed to see a white woman cleaning a bathroom there. It was the first time she had seen it in her life."

Olive shook her head and smiled at Shannon, encouraging her on.

"So, being in California is good for us. It's showing us how everyone has equal value in the sight of God. In South Africa, some places were dangerous for the black people, and other places were dangerous for us as white people. Mom and Dad thought the school systems were getting corrupt as well, with bringing in evolution. So that's why we left."

"But schools in America teach evolution too," Olive told Shannon.

"They do. Mom and Dad found out that the United States is actually more liberal than South Africa. But there is more freedom to homeschool here. And we're with you." Shannon gave Olive a friendly nod.

Once again, Olive decided she was glad she lived in the desert of Frazier Park. If Eli Glick's church people could brave the hardships of an unknown culture, surely she could learn to be happy with the state she had grown up in. Would the Herr family have found anyone who shared their concerns if the Anabaptist church weren't here? And if the Brennemans hadn't moved to California, Olive would have never met Shannon.

chapter eleven

THE SUMMER THAT OLIVE TURNED THIRTEEN was exciting and busy for the Brennemans. Mom had just had a new baby, a girl named Kristen. One day at lunchtime Dad told Mom, "I just had a phone call from Andy Brubacher."

Olive perked up her ears. Andy called Dad now and then to talk about his work with orphanages in Mexico. This was the second year Andy planned to take a group of Anabaptist singles and young people to Mexico. They would spend a week helping in orphanages close to the city of Tijuana. Tijuana was on the Mexican border, only a four-hour drive from Frazier Park. Sometimes Dad helped Andy with legal work that could be taken care of in California. But why was Dad bringing up Andy's call now?

"I see. What did he want?" Mom asked.

"He wanted to know if we would consent to cook for the

group that's coming to Tijuana this year."

"Well!" Mom said, sounding startled. "That would be a big job for this family, wouldn't it?"

Dad had taken a big bite of his sandwich, so that silenced him for quite a while. Finally he answered. "I thought so too, but Andy seems to think we are the perfect ones to do it. I told him that we have a brand new baby, but he pointed out that the group isn't coming until January. I told him we'd consider it."

Olive looked at Mom holding the baby. After Kristen was born, it had been kind of sad to think that there was nothing big to look forward to. Now wouldn't it be grand if they could anticipate a week in Mexico! The Brennemans had never been to Mexico, except for a brief visit across the border when Uncle Joshua's family had visited California a few years before.

"I hope we go," Madeline said, and the rest agreed.

"One thing is certain," Mom broke in, "I won't even consider it if Aunt Marge isn't willing to go along. If I have to cook, I'll need someone to help with the children."

Dad thought of something else. "Andy said we would probably need to choose another person or young couple to help cook."

Mom looked thoughtful. "It just might be possible if we had enough help. You know, I would be thrilled to cook for them if the details were taken care of."

"Are we details?" Sandra asked seriously, and then she looked almost like she could cry when her brothers and sisters laughed.

"It's okay," Dad said, picking up Sandra and putting her on his knee. "You actually are a detail, in a way—a nice detail that makes our life more interesting."

Sandra smiled at them and decided not to worry about it. The rest of the children kept talking about Mexico.

It took a week for Dad and Mom to decide for sure. Aunt Marge was happy to go along to take care of the children, and an older single lady from church, Christine Perkins, agreed to help cook. So Dad called Andy back and told him they would do it.

Mom spent quite a bit of time planning her menu, but two weeks before the Brennemans were scheduled to leave, Mom had a surprise. Andy informed Dad that the kitchen they would be using would be a motel room.

"What?" Mom asked when Dad told her that useful piece of information. She was shocked. "How on earth am I supposed to cook for seventy-five people in a motel room?"

"You heard right," said Dad. "He said we have to use big roasters and electric skillets to heat things and ice chests to keep things cold. We have to get groceries every day."

"I wanted to make a lot of things ahead of time," Mom mourned, but then she brightened up. "We'll just do what we have to do. If somebody could do it last year, then I guess we can do it too."

The Brenneman van was packed like a can of sardines by the time they were ready to leave for Mexico. Andy had sent some money for supplies, and Mom had borrowed various items from the church ladies. Christine Perkins and

Aunt Marge followed the Brenneman van in Christine's car, loaded with the food Mom had been able to buy.

The van was full of excitement as the Brennemans headed south to San Diego. Even Zachary, who was almost two, was jabbering in order to fit in with his chattering siblings.

The trip was normal until they reached the city of Chula Vista, south of San Diego. Here they would cross the border into Mexico. Olive had butterflies in her stomach as they slowed down to wait their turn.

"Don't worry," Dad said. "No one even checks you out very much heading into Mexico. It's crossing into the United States that can be tough."

"Why's that?" Leonard wondered. "It seems turned around from the way it ought to be. Since we're U.S. citizens, shouldn't the government be worried about us escaping to Mexico?"

Dad shook his head. "That's not how it works. They know that if a U.S. citizen goes to Mexico, it's probably just for a visit. But they worry that Mexican people who aren't U.S. citizens will enter the United States and stay here. See, we can visit Mexico with just our birth certificates, but the Mexicans can't visit the United States like that."

"That's not fair," Olive said.

"No, it's not," Dad agreed. "But that's how it is. The problem is that our country is the richer country, and our government thinks that if the Mexicans visit us, they might not go back home."

"They just keep right on visiting for the rest of their lives,"

Leonard said to clarify Dad's statement.

"Then how do so many Mexicans come to California anyway?" Madeline wondered.

"They sneak in," Dad explained. "Lots and lots of them. A lot of Americans are glad they do, because the Americans like their work. Americans don't really want to have to pick the grapes in the valley and do all the other jobs that require working out in the hot sun. Usually they're glad the Mexicans are willing to do them. The Mexicans are happy for the jobs, even if they don't pay very well. They're still making more money than they could make in Mexico, and a lot of them are sending money home to their families."

"I like Mexicans," Andrea declared from the middle seat. "I think it's very kind of them to work in the hot sun and then send the money home."

"Mexicans are usually friendly," Mom said, "and eager to please. I hope we can be that way in their country. Of course it's hard to be friendly when we can hardly speak a word of Spanish. But we can smile."

There was an immediate change in the road when the van crossed to the other side of the border. Right away the pavement was bumpy, and there was trash along the road. The children grew silent as they stared at the many beggars along the street.

"Shall we give them something?" whispered Madeline, but Dad kept on driving. They were heading into downtown Tijuana, and Olive had never heard such honking! It seemed that in Mexico people used their horns to express their emotions instead of using them in emergencies like people in the States did.

Olive took it all in—the dirty water by the side of the road, the throngs of people, and the bright colors that Mexicans love. Every time Dad stopped at an intersection, there were people selling things. They ran right up to his window and begged Dad to buy their wares. Dad got tired of shaking his head and learned to just look straight ahead, as though he were too busy driving to look around.

Mom read the directions, and Dad was trying to turn at the correct places, but it was hard to keep your bearings with all the beeping cars and general confusion of Tijuana. Olive began to worry that they might end up at the wrong place.

"Look at that," said Leonard, pointing just ahead. It was a zebra, standing calmly on the street corner, waiting for someone to ride it.

Olive's mouth dropped open. "I thought zebras couldn't be tamed!"

"They can't normally," said Mom, "so something's funny about that one. We'll have to ask Andy how the Mexicans tame zebras."

After what seemed like hours of bumping on the Tijuana streets, they finally reached the edge of town where the traffic was thinner and the air less stifling. There they found the motel. Andy Brubacher was there to greet them and assure them they were at the right place.

The Brennemans milled around and watched as load after

load of singles and young people pulled into the parking lot. Mom was busy getting her cold supper ready, and it wasn't long before darkness blanketed the land. Andy showed the Brennemans their rooms and gave them strict orders not to drink the water from the faucets or even use it to brush their teeth. If they did, they might get sick.

Olive looked around at the girls' room. It was clean and orderly and looked a lot like motel rooms in the United States. Olive was surprised. She thought sleeping in Mexico would be kind of rough, but who could tell the difference?

They all noticed a difference, though, during the night. Young men in Mexico liked cars without mufflers, and they also liked to drive them most of the night. Olive kept waking up to the loud roar of yet another car, leaving her tired and frustrated by morning. This was life in Mexico!

In the morning Aunt Marge bustled about, dressing and combing girls and getting Zachary ready for the day. Olive wondered how Mom and Dad were getting along, trying to get breakfast and take care of Kristen. At least they had Christine to help them! Olive poked her head into the "kitchen" and saw them busily working on temporary tables. They had scrambled eggs, and now they were frying bread to make toast, since there was no toaster.

After breakfast, Dad wondered if Leonard and Olive wanted to go with him to get groceries. Of course they did. Andy explained that there was an authentic Mexican grocery store within a mile, but if they went farther into the city, they could find exactly the same type of grocery store they went to in Bakersfield, California. Another surprise!

Dad decided to go to the American one first. Away they went, back into the honking, congested traffic. At the grocery store, Dad had some problems. He couldn't find everything he needed, and he knew almost no Spanish. Finally he addressed a worker.

"No English," said the worker.

Dad tried another one. "No English," came the reply again.

Well, maybe the third worker would know English.

"Do you know where I can get cornmeal?" Dad asked.

The worker shook his head. "What you call cornmeal is not a Mexican food, and you can't get it here," he said in perfect English. What a relief! At least Dad could talk to someone without using sign language.

"Now I'm surprised," Dad said. "I would have thought Mexico was the very place where people do eat cornmeal."

"We do eat a lot of corn tortillas, but they're made with something called masa," the worker explained. "It's a lot like cornmeal, but not the same. It's made from dried corn that was treated with lime."

"I see," said Dad. "I'll take your word for it, because I can tell you know more about these things than I do." Dad laughed heartily, and the friendly Mexican laughed with him.

The Brennemans went on down the aisle. But now they couldn't find the butter.

Dad was getting bolder. He asked a customer standing

by, "Do you speak English?"

"Some," said the man.

"Do you know where the butter is?"

"Sure. It's over there," he said, pointing. The man seemed to know more than just a little English.

At the checkout counter, Leonard punched Olive. "Look at the bag boys. They're wee little." Sure enough, they looked like they were no more than ten or eleven years old. But they were working hard, bagging groceries. After Dad paid the clerk, the bag boy looked at him eagerly, but the Brennemans took their bags and walked way. As they headed to the van, Olive was thinking.

"Dad, do you think we were supposed to tip that bag boy?" she asked.

Dad looked at Olive. "I wonder if you're right, now that I think about it," he said. "I think I did see a lady give the bag boy money. I guess it never entered my head that I was expected to pay for something that we think is part of the store's job."

Next there was a friendly Mexican offering to help put their groceries in the van. *Everybody is so kind and helpful in Mexico*, Olive was thinking. Dad shook his head. He had two able-bodied children to help him. The man looked sad and walked away. That's when Olive realized it again—he wanted a tip.

"What's going on?" Leonard asked out loud. "Does everybody get paid to do normal things around here?"

Dad smiled, "I guess that's the way the poor survive here.

In America poor people get money from the government, but since they don't have that here, the poor people probably rely on tips to live."

Olive had felt a little angry at all the people who wanted money from them, but she started feeling more compassionate. *Those poor little bag boys are trying to help their mothers. In the United States they wouldn't even be allowed to work, but here they probably don't have any other choice.*

Dad stopped at the Spanish store on the way home to get ice. It took some time to find someone who knew English, because poor Dad didn't even know the Spanish word for ice. Once he heard it, he decided they should memorize that one since they were going to be buying a lot of ice for the ice chest.

When Olive and Leonard left the store, they were practicing the new word. *"Hielo.* It sounds like 'yellow,' " Olive said. "Next time we'll just tell them we want 'yellow.' "

"That's it!" agreed Andy later at the motel while they were gathering for supper. "The Spanish word for ice sounds very similar to 'yellow.' "

"Hey, Andy," Olive said, suddenly remembering the zebra, "how do Mexicans tame their zebras?"

Andy looked amused, but it was time to pray, so he had to wait to answer. And after prayer he was so busy arranging things that he forgot Olive's question.

Wednesday was Mom and Dad's anniversary, and Andy gave them some good news.

"We're invited to a Christian community in the mountains for supper tonight, so you won't have to make supper. Why don't you all take the day off to do some sightseeing?"

Dad liked that idea, and as soon as the pancake mess was cleaned up from breakfast, they were all packed in the van. Aunt Marge and Christine Perkins went along to help with the younger children, and Olive was glad for that. Otherwise she would've had to spend a lot of her time getting drinks for the little ones, soothing Kristen in her seat, and all the other things that Mom couldn't do because she was buckled in.

Madeline thought of something. "I wonder if we even have to be in car seats and seat belts in Mexico."

"It doesn't matter," said Dad. "We'll wear them anyway."

After they had driven a while, the city gave way to the countryside, but what was that on the left? The Brennemans all craned their necks to see. It looked like a great hillside of junk with boards, plastic, and trash. There were people there, sitting in the sunshine. "These are the slums," Christine explained, since she had been in Mexico before. "Those are people's houses."

The Brennemans were too shocked for words. Why, those things looked nothing like houses! They were only pieces of junk with plastic on top. Mangy dogs wandered around, and wrinkled, grizzled people sat by the piles of junk.

As they drove away from the slums, Olive was deep in thought. To think that she complained about anything, ever, made her feel guilty. She wondered what those poor folks had to eat. Maybe nothing sometimes. And the dirt! How would it be never to have a real bath? Olive had never realized until her trip to Mexico that being clean was a privilege that not everyone had. Even the streets of Tijuana were dirty and dusty. One couldn't stay clean long, even if he left home that way.

"I guess we have it pretty nice," said Andrea, breaking the silence.

"I know," Leonard agreed. "Maybe we should try to make money for those people somehow."

"You may," said Christine, "but for most of them, that is the only life they've ever known. Because no one has ever taught them, they don't know how to use money wisely. If they get money, they often spend it on alcohol to drown out their misery."

"Ooooooh no!" exclaimed the Brenneman children. That was worse yet.

"What they really need," declared Madeline, "is to know God."

"That is certainly right," agreed Christine. "That is the place to start."

Now the Brenneman van drove beside the ocean. It was a beautiful, sunny day, and the ocean was just as picturesque in Mexico as in California. Soon they reached their destination, a small tourist town called Roserita. Everyone tumbled out of the van, and Dad did a head count once they were all rounded up to make sure no one was still sleeping in the van. Mom wanted to shop, so they entered a Mexican mall.

The mall had lots of small shacks covered with big tarps. All of the shacks were filled with merchandise. Everything was so brightly colored and gaudy, and it was a full-time job to keep Sandra, Florence, and Zachary from touching things. Mom looked at some beautiful, thick blankets, but the lady named an enormous sum of money.

Mom shook her head.

"What you give?" the lady asked eagerly.

"I will give you twenty dollars," Mom told her. The lady shook her head with a disgusted look.

"No, no," she said. "Fifty."

Mom shook her head and moved on. The lady followed them. "T'irty-five," she said, pleading with her eyes. Mom shook her head and moved on. Leonard was interested in the leather exhibit, and Dad was thinking of allowing him to buy a wallet. But again, there was frustration about the price. Dad had made up his mind that Leonard wouldn't pay more than seven dollars, and the man asked for twelve.

"Seven," Dad offered and moved on. The man seemed almost angry as they left.

Mom tried to buy a couple more things, but the prices were too high. Even children's sunglasses cost way too much.

"Don't they realize that we can buy them cheaper in the United States?" Mom asked Dad as they left.

"I don't know," Dad said. "I think maybe we expect to get things cheaper because we're in Mexico, and they expect us to pay more because we're from the United States."

Next it was lunch time. There was a little restaurant close by, and the whole Brenneman troop went in to give them some business.

The menu was simple, just like the Mexican restaurant at home, and the Brennemans even knew what they wanted to eat—tacos! The waiter was eager to please them, but they ran into some problems. Mom wanted a high chair for Zachary, but the waiter couldn't understand her gestures.

"Tell him you want a *silla*," whispered Leonard.

Mom tried her best, but the waiter was baffled. So Aunt Marge held Zachary while she tried to eat. The tacos were delicious except for one thing. They were too spicy-hot. The adults were able to manage them, but the children took a few bites and suddenly weren't hungry anymore.

"This is Mexico," explained Aunt Marge. "We should've told them, 'No salsa!'"

"But would they have understood us?" asked Mom. "I'll tell you, if there's one thing this trip is teaching me, it is to have compassion on all the Hispanics at home who can't speak English well."

"I know," agreed Dad. "We tend to think they're a little simple when they can't talk to us, and now I feel like the simple one."

The children slept most of the way back to the motel, and Mom and Dad had a relaxing time visiting with Aunt Marge and Christine. As soon as they got back, Andy told them to get ready to head to the mountains for supper.

It was dark most of the way, so Olive didn't see too much

as they drove. But she could feel that they were steadily climbing. Olive wondered how different this mountain community was from the mountain community where she lived.

It took over an hour to get to their destination, and the last few miles were on a bumpy mountain road. Some smiling Mexicans welcomed them into a small shed, where they had tables set up. They had paper plates laid out for all of them, and the tables were long enough to seat everyone. Olive wondered if these people were wealthier than the average Mexicans, or if they had spent half a year's wages to feed the group.

Supper was simple, just hunks of chicken breast, plain white rice, and fruit. The shed was cold, and Olive shivered. How could the young people who were visiting at the orphanage just keep eating and talking as if it wasn't frigid in the shed? Mom had gathered every blanket she had in the van for the little ones, but there were simply not enough for Olive. Once again Olive felt the helplessness of the poor people. No matter how much she wanted a heater, there were no heaters to be had.

It was a strange visit with lots of smiles but not much fellowship. Andy knew Spanish well, as did a couple of the visiting young people, so they talked to their hosts. Then Andy announced that they would sing.

The Brennemans joined the other visitors in singing English songs to their Mexican hosts. The folks there seemed mightily pleased, and they smiled and clapped. Then Andy asked the Mexicans to sing to them in Spanish. They were happy to oblige, and they sang beautiful songs. Olive could tell they were Christian songs because they often sang the Spanish words for God and Jesus and love, which were some of the few Spanish words she knew.

Olive was so cold that she couldn't really enjoy anything. She was so glad to be tucked away in the van once again for the journey home. After finally warming up, she slept the whole way back to the hotel.

It was unbelievable how fast the week passed. Saturday was a free day for the youth, and Andy encouraged the Brennemans to poke around Tijuana too. Once again they tried to shop in the hustle and bustle of the city and its bright wares. This time they discovered what they had been doing wrong earlier. Andy told them the locals would get angry if their customers didn't barter with them.

"When the Mexicans come to the United States, we expect them to learn to buy things the way we normally sell them, right? Well, when we come to their country, we need to barter. If we don't, we seem totally unworkable to them. Give them a low price and go up a little to what you want to pay. They will be much happier with you."

And they were. Dad bought a suitcase and a leather three-legged stool. Mom bought a leather purse and a few coin purses for the children.

On Sunday morning the church service was held at a park in Tijuana. It seemed that half of Tijuana had come to the park too, but for a different reason. They were having a

Sunday morning party. Olive had never seen such festivity before. There were piñatas and sticks with grilled meat for sale. Lots of men with guitars added swingy, Latino music to the party.

Church was held in a large gazebo, and Andy preached. Olive could hardly keep her mind on the service with all the festivities around them. The smell of barbequing made her hungry. Andy was talking about the work in Mexico. "We feel like we can't do much in a week," he said, "but if we touch one life, it will be worth it."

Olive thought about the needs in the slums. *Maybe if the orphans are helped, they will feel the love of Jesus, and when they're older, they'll be Christians and preach to the folks in the slums.*

After the service, their group grilled hamburgers and had their own cookout in the park. Olive felt rich to bite into a burger, after thinking about the slums. Suddenly she remembered something else.

"Andy," she said, "about the zebras."

"Oh, yes," Andy replied, "I never answered you. Those are not zebras; they're carefully painted ponies. The Mexicans love to do that."

Andy turned to Dad. "So what did you think of your week in Mexico?"

"It was a learning experience for sure," Dad told him. "I enjoyed it, but I'm looking forward to getting back to a place where they speak my language. And where people don't expect to be paid for helping me park."

Andy chuckled, "Yes, it takes a while to get used to the system. When you see all the handicapped people begging on the streets, you have to remember they have no other way to survive."

"I had some stress getting the sliced ham for supper the other night," Dad said. "They had to sell it to me in kilograms, and I had no idea how much to get. Then they wouldn't believe me when I managed to convert it. They thought I was just a dumb American who didn't know how much I wanted."

"That's interesting," laughed Andy. "I guess the size of our group shocked them. Yes, there are some challenges in learning to deal with other cultures for sure. But I do like Mexican culture. The people are friendly and pleasant."

Dad nodded. "They can teach us a lot of lessons. We tend to be more independent and cold, don't we?"

Getting through the border back into the United States was a long, drawn-out affair. The Brennemans waited in line two hours and looked at all the vendors trying to sell ponchos, sombreros, and trinkets of all kinds. Among them were beggars wanting money for nothing at all. Dad remembered Andy's explanation of the system, and he gave quarters to them until he had no more quarters. Then there were the food vendors. The food looked and smelled so good, but Dad didn't buy any because it was Sunday. At least that made it easy for Dad!

Olive felt nervous when it was actually their turn to cross the border. What if the border officer didn't trust Dad or

Christine Perkins behind them? The gruff officer looked them over and asked Dad if they were bringing back any Mexican goods. When Dad explained that they had bought only a few souvenirs, the officer waved them on. They were on the way to San Diego.

Now the road was smooth and wide. Everything was clean and landscaped. Olive had never realized how clean the United States was and how well the roads were maintained. As they sailed along, they passed a sign that told them to watch for fugitives crossing the highway. Olive felt a great pity for those poor folks who were so desperate to leave Mexico that they were willing to risk their lives. She was sure she would look at the Mexican Americans in a whole new light, now that she had spent some time in their country. They were people just like her.

chapter twelve

"I CAN'T BELIEVE IT," OLIVE SAID FOR THE fourth time in five minutes.

Leonard nodded gravely. "It takes a while for your brain to digest news like that."

Dad just stood there without saying anything. Aunt Judy had just called and told them that Miguel Juarez had been killed in a car accident the night before. Miguel, the young man from El Salvador, the one who was always smiling, was gone—just like that.

Olive thought about the last time she had seen Miguel. He was sitting in church, doing his best to sing in English. The Sunday before he had given a confession about some bad attitudes he was struggling with and a testimony of how he had found victory over them. It was hard for Olive to imagine that Miguel could have bad attitudes, with his eternal smile, but that was another lesson for life. Just because someone acted happy didn't mean he never had struggles. Now Olive was so glad Miguel had taken care of that so he was ready to die!

"What happened?" Mom asked at last.

"I don't know," Dad answered. "Aunt Judy just said that he didn't show up to work with Uncle Craig this morning, and another worker finally called and told Uncle Craig the news."

Dad's phone rang, and it was Abram Miller, making sure the church people had heard the news. Dad asked some questions, and Olive was anxious to hear the story.

"It was on Wheeler Ridge Road," Dad explained after he hung up with Abram. "A car missed the bend and crashed right into Miguel's car. He died instantly."

"Oh, his poor mother," Mom said sadly. "He was her only son. I wish for her sake that she could be here for the funeral."

Dad had to go to work in spite of the sudden turn of events, so life went on for the Brennemans. When the other church people tried to plan the funeral, they began to realize that in Salvadoran culture, even distant relatives are considered family. The relatives all wanted to be involved, so the church let them plan most of the funeral. After all, the church people couldn't even speak the language Miguel spoke most of the time.

"They're planning to send the body to El Salvador?" Olive wasn't sure she had heard right. How could that be done? Didn't bodies deteriorate when they were dead? But

Olive had heard correctly. The modern embalming process allowed enough time to have a funeral in the States and then fly the body home to Miguel's mother. Olive was glad for his mother's sake. She couldn't imagine how it would be to have your only son die far away in another country.

The funeral was held in Bakersfield, right in town. The Brennemans felt sober as they walked into the funeral home. There was a long line to view the body, and Olive felt all mixed up. She wanted to see Miguel, yet she didn't. When the Brenneman family's turn came, Olive was surprised how much Miguel looked just like himself. There were gloves on his hands, to hide the effects of the accident, and Olive saw that if she looked closely at his hair, there was a great big line of stitches hiding in there. Poor Miguel!

They all sat down on the padded seats and waited for the service to begin. Miguel's relatives hadn't chosen any preacher but had wanted the church to find one. Where could they find an Anabaptist preacher who spoke Spanish? A church three hours north did have a minister who had grown up in Costa Rica, so he agreed to come down and preach.

It seemed strange to listen to the preacher speaking in a different language, but Olive thought it sounded beautiful. Steve Mueller spoke for an hour, and then Carlos Hernández opened the service for anyone else who wanted to speak. A non-Christian co-worker of Miguel's spoke for a few minutes, and Olive wished she could understand what he was saying. Then family members spoke, all in Spanish.

A few of the church brethren told stories in English about working with Miguel.

Finally Carlos Hernández took the microphone again. He had a Bible in his hand as he spoke. He spoke Spanish first and then translated what he had said into English.

Carlos had been a good friend of Miguel, since they spoke the same language and went to the same church, and he wanted to tell the congregation what he found in Miguel's car after the accident. While he was talking, he suddenly opened the Bible, showing that it was streaked with blood. Everyone gasped, and the family members began shrieking and wailing.

Olive felt weak. It was awful to see that Bible. And yet it was special to know that it was in the car with Miguel at the accident. Carlos said that it had been right beside Miguel on the seat when he died. Carlos talked for a while, encouraging the listeners to follow Miguel's example, and then he sat down.

Next the funeral director led them outside for a "dove release." Olive wondered what that meant. She had never seen such a thing before. The funeral director and family had arranged for some loud music to be played, and Olive's ears cringed at the sound. It sounded so unholy after such a solemn service. But the words were actually fitting, and Olive tried to think about them.

The director explained that the doves he had in his cage were trained to return to their master, and when he released them, they would go home, just as a soul returns to God.

Then he opened the cage and let the birds go.

While the music thumped on, with words about soaring to the Master, the doves circled the sky above the funeral home and then disappeared in the sky. The music stopped, and all was quiet.

The church people from Lebec then all drove to the church. Miguel's family had wanted to share a meal with them. Olive was looking forward to tasting Salvadoran food, although she wasn't hungry after such a solemn service.

There were tamales for supper. Olive had often wished she could eat an authentic tamale since the ones in the grocery story were an American version of the real thing. She and Shannon Herr found a place in the food line, and Olive realized that she was hungry after all. The ladies were very helpful, even if most of them talked only Spanish, and Olive got her tamale.

She had taken two big bites when Shannon tapped her on the shoulder. "Be careful," she warned, "there are bones in there."

Olive looked at her tamale. It looked so delicious with its corn dough around the meat and vegetables. It must have been a mistake that there was a bone in Shannon's. But no, the third bite of hers had a bone too. Did Salvadorans eat bones? Surely not. Well, they must have gotten used to eating carefully and pulling out the bones. The tamale was good anyway, and the sweet buns afterward were a treat.

Olive listened to an English-speaking cousin of Miguel's talking to Mom.

"Miguel's mother watched the service on the internet at the library in El Salvador," the cousin explained. "I just talked to her on the phone since the service ended."

"How nice!" Mom said. "It's a modern world we live in."

"She was feeling very sad," the cousin continued, "because the last she saw of her boy was before he ran away from home to sneak to America. She was worried about his soul. Had he really made everything right? But then when Carlos showed his Bible, she felt peace."

"And do you know," said the cousin, "Miguel was helping his mom start a business in El Salvador. He was sending part of his earnings home to her. Now she won't be able to start the business."

Olive saw tears in the cousin's eyes and in Mom's eyes too. If only they could comfort Miguel's mom in some way. And that's when the idea came to Olive. They could make her a scrapbook in Spanish. That would be fun! It seemed like such a little thing, but maybe it would help.

The Brennemans sat around that evening and talked about the day.

"I didn't like seeing a dead person," said Florence. "Why do we look at them?"

"It's good for us," said Dad. "It helps us to believe the person really died, and it also helps us to think about heaven."

"That reminds me of a Bible verse we learned in our schoolwork last year," Leonard said. "It's in Ecclesiastes. It says, 'It is better to go to the house of mourning, than to go to the house of feasting.' "

"It is more beneficial to our souls," agreed Mom. "Death is a part of life. It helps us remember eternity, but I'm surely glad we don't have to face it as often as the pioneers did." Mom looked around thankfully at her family.

Olive was listening with her pen poised above her paper. She was writing down a list of people whom she would ask to help fix a scrapbook.

It was only two months later when Olive found an excellent way to send her scrapbook to Miguel's mother. Carlos Hernández was going to El Salvador to visit her. The scrapbook had just been completed, and Olive couldn't wait to see if Miguel's mother would like it. Carlos had done a lot of translating for them, and Olive was pleased at how the people worked to make the pages beautiful and inspiring.

Carlos was gone for two weeks, and the Brennemans invited him for supper two nights after he returned.

"Oh, Olive," Carlos exclaimed the minute he walked in the door, "I have to tell you how much Miguel's mother liked your scrapbook. She just cried and cried with gratitude."

Olive felt little warm spirals twisting all around her heart. She had actually helped to comfort Miguel's mom! She was glad for all the time she had spent making her page and talking to other people about making the book.

"She couldn't believe you made her book in Spanish, and she was so grateful. She wanted me to make sure to tell the people here thank you," Carlos continued.

As they all sat around and ate, Carlos had another

story for them. "You know, I almost died down there in El Salvador," he said.

The Brennemans were all ears.

"Yes," Carlos went on, "I almost died. Miguel's mother and some of her church family decided to take me to the ocean one day while I was there. And I wanted to swim. Now I'm a good swimmer." Carlos looked around the table. The family was all listening intently.

"I swam out into the ocean," Carlos continued. "Well, the tide was going out, and I ended up swimming a little farther than I should've, and it was pretty deep out there. Suddenly I realized that I was very tired. Swimming is hard work, and I'm not really in shape anymore." Carlos paused and looked down at his ample stomach. "Anyway, I started swimming toward shore with all my might, but I just couldn't get very far. And every wave would take me back a little ways, out to sea. I really thought my life on earth was over."

Dad looked at Carlos incredulously. "But you're here with us," he said. "How did you get to shore?"

"I gained a little ground," continued Carlos. "I got close enough to shore that I could touch bottom and then jump up and get some air. I did that for a little bit. I was so tired that I thought I couldn't swim, but I was able to wave to the folks on the shore, to tell them I needed help. They just waved back."

Olive held her breath. She wanted Carlos to hurry and finish the story so she could relax again.

"I knew this was my last chance," Carlos said, "so I prayed and used all the strength I had, which wasn't much, I tell you. I made it a few yards to where I could stand in the water and breathe. I don't think I've ever been so beat out in all my life."

"Praise God!" said Dad. "Your life was saved for a purpose, Carlos."

"I know," agreed Carlos, "and I was sure glad I didn't need to make another funeral for Miguel's mother."

"I agree, poor woman!" said Mom heartily, and the talk changed to other things. Olive sat thinking about the scrapbook. This was the first time she had been in charge of something that was such a blessing to a hurting soul. It was the first time she had personally felt what Mom had been telling her, about the most important things in life. Helping a hurting person was much more satisfying than anything else she had ever done.

chapter thirteen

"NOW THIS YEAR," SAID MOM, "WE'RE going to have a real garden. At the old house, the soil was too poor, and there was hardly enough land to make one. And last year the garden didn't do well because it was the first year we tried it here."

"You really think you'll be happier with a garden?" Dad asked, grinning in a fatherly way at Mom.

Mom had to defend herself. "Well, I've been happy for ten years without one, but don't you think God would want us to raise our own food if we can?"

"I suppose," Dad agreed.

"Last year was a good try," Mom said. "But it was our first year, and we didn't know a thing about watering. This year . . ."

". . . we're going to do it right." Dad finished Mom's sentence.

"Exactly."

The next Saturday Dad made an announcement. "Leonard, you and I are going to go manure shopping."

Olive laughed. What in the world was Dad talking about?

"For the garden, you know," Dad explained. "I have no idea how to get manure for it unless we go down to the farms and shop for it. I mean, we'll just ask the farm workers until someone lets me have a load or two."

"May I go along?" shouted all the little girls at once, hanging on to Dad like drowning children. Dad looked down at his little girls and smiled.

"Well, it's nice to be so popular," he said. "I have many admirers this morning." The sarcasm went unheeded, and the girls only shouted louder.

Mom put her hands over her ears and made the girls be quiet. They quieted down, but they still hung on to Dad. "I think I will take Leonard and the only girl who was quiet," said Dad, looking at Olive who was sitting primly on a chair at the table. She was past the stage of shouting when she wanted to go with Dad. But she was beaming inside as she went to get her socks and shoes. It was special to go on a drive with Dad and Leonard.

It was half-an-hour's drive to the farms. They were actually more like milk factories than farms, with herds ranging from five thousand to twenty thousand cows. They all had plenty of manure, but the problem was finding someone in charge who could give them permission to take some. Dad had brought some shovels, but he was sure hoping a worker would load his trailer with their equipment.

At the first farm they couldn't find anyone around who was the boss, so they went on to the second. They had more success there. A friendly Hispanic told them to take all they wanted from a big pile of barnyard scrapings of sawdust and manure. Dad was pleased because that was just what he wanted. The man even loaded it with a little skid loader, so just like that they were ready to head home. The man didn't charge for the manure, but Dad gave him ten dollars.

While Dad was talking to the man, Olive and Leonard looked at the row of cows eating. For as far as they could see, there were cows with their heads through the bars, eating what was on the other side. When Dad was finished talking, Leonard begged for a chance to watch the milking. Dad walked with them to the huge milk house. There were some tall tanks that looked like silos from the East, and Dad said those were the bulk tanks for the fresh milk.

Olive never got bored watching cows being milked. At these farms, the cows took a ride as they were being milked. Somehow they knew when it was their turn to step onto the "merry-go-round" where the milkers were. The machine rotated very slowly, and by the time it came around to the place where the cow had gotten on, the cow had been milked and knew that it was time to back off the machine.

Olive compared it to the barn in Ohio where Uncle Conrad worked, and she had to admit this was faster. Yet she preferred Uncle Conrad's way. You wouldn't have named a cow Franky, like Uncle Conrad did, in a California dairy.

Here each cow seemed the same as the next one, and there was no personal connection at all.

Dad got two trailer loads of manure that day, and he made a big pile on Mom's garden spot. He had done a lot of work the year before to dig a ditch around the garden and put chicken wire down in it so that the ground squirrels couldn't dig their way into the garden. Then he brought several dump truck loads of topsoil from Lebec, where the soil was better.

"Why do the wild animals eat things so quickly out here?" Mom had wondered.

Dad's explanation was simple. "In Ohio there are plenty of green fields to eat, but in California, when the ground squirrels and the rabbits find a nice green spot, they run to tell their friends."

Mom had nodded and sighed. "I guess having a garden is expensive here," she said. "It sure is different than Ohio. But no," Mom caught herself. "I don't want to teach my children that my home community was best. I want them to feel at home here and appreciate the different advantages and beauties we have. So we will learn to garden the California way!"

"Maybe we won't have as many weeds," Madeline suggested, and Mom patted her on the shoulder.

"That's it. We need to look for things that are better here."

The Brennemans had to spread the manure by hand, and they were tired of it long before they were done. Finally they were ready to plant.

"I wouldn't plant quite yet," Dad cautioned. "It's only the beginning of May."

Mom patiently waited a few more weeks, and then what fun they had planting! Olive was excited. After all the work they had done, she was confident that this year things would grow.

Sure enough, the seeds obediently came up, and in a few weeks there were beautiful rows of corn, green beans, and red beets. Then came the cold weather. Olive looked at the thermometer worriedly before they went to bed, and then at Dad, as if he might be able to do something.

"I'm going to bed," Dad yawned. "I can't do a thing about the weather, and we might as well not lose sleep over it."

"Well, you could be sympathetic," Olive told him. "Think of all the hard work we put into that garden."

When Olive looked out the window the next morning, she saw a thin blanket of snow over the earth. She couldn't believe her eyes. Snow! Of all the years to have snow at the end of May!

Mom was matter of fact about it. "Well, we can't change it now. Maybe it will pull through anyway."

It did pull through, after a fashion, and Mom and Leonard poured fertilizer water over all the plants. But they never thrived. It seemed that the soil was still too poor. The tomato plants just sat there, balking at growing new leaves.

"I declare," Mom said. "We might need to grow things in pure manure. Well, if we never can raise a good garden, we'll just find other things to like about living in California."

* * * *

One bright and sunny day Mom decided to take the older children to the museum in Frazier Park. Aunt Marge agreed to watch the little children, and Mom took the oldest three to the museum. It was interesting to see pictures of the first ranches in the area and to find out that the town had been started as a gold-mining town.

"Did you know a lot of the coastal towns were started as Catholic missions?" asked the guide in the museum.

Olive was surprised. She hadn't realized that Catholics had migrated west to start missions.

"Oh, yes," Mom said, seeing Olive's surprise. "Some of the first men who braved the Great American Desert were Catholic missionaries. They tried to convert the Indians to Christianity, and they did convert some."

The guide was nodding. "The problem was they thought that as a part of their conversion the Indians needed to adapt to American culture, and often the Indians weren't happy. The missionaries gave them American clothes and tried to make houses for them on the mission grounds. But that wasn't the Indian way."

Olive thought that was strange. Why couldn't the Indians be Christians and still live like Indians?

"But that wasn't how Frazier Park was started, you know," the lady continued. "Frazier Park was a gold-mining town, and our neighboring town of Gorman was a roadside rest stop. Fort Tejon protected the area."

"Would you look at that!" Mom exclaimed as she studied

about the AUTHOR

FONDA GOOD WAS BORN INTO A LOVING Christian home in Wayne County, Ohio, and grew up with four brothers and one sister. Her love of writing began when she was a girl in school; composition class was her favorite. At the age of twenty, she married Bruce, a godly young man who was also her neighbor, and he has been a great help in her spiritual journey.

Fonda always hoped to have a big family, and God granted her childhood dream by giving her and her husband ten children, with many accompanying challenges and blessings. For recreation, Fonda writes, but she also finds great enjoyment in homeschooling her children, quilting, and many other tasks of homemaking and motherhood.

Fonda welcomes reader response and can be contacted at brucegood@integrity.com. You may also write to her in care of Christian Aid Ministries, P.O. Box 360, Berlin, Ohio 44610.

Christian Aid Ministries

CHRISTIAN AID MINISTRIES WAS FOUNDED in 1981 as a nonprofit, tax-exempt 501(c)(3) organization. Its primary purpose is to provide a trustworthy and efficient channel for Amish, Mennonite, and other conservative Anabaptist groups and individuals to minister to physical and spiritual needs around the world. This is in response to the command ". . . do good unto all men, especially unto them who are of the household of faith" (Gal. 6:10).

Each year, CAM supporters provide approximately 15 million pounds of food, clothing, medicines, seeds, Bibles, Bible story books, and other Christian literature for needy people. Most of the aid goes to orphans and Christian families. Supporters' funds also help clean up and rebuild for natural disaster victims, put up Gospel billboards in the U.S., support several church-planting efforts, operate two medical clinics, and provide resources for needy families to make their own living. CAM's main purposes for providing aid are to help and encourage God's people and bring the Gospel to a lost and dying world.

CAM has staff, warehouse, and distribution networks in Romania, Moldova, Ukraine, Haiti, Nicaragua, Liberia, and Israel. Aside from management, supervisory personnel, and bookkeeping operations, volunteers do most of the work at CAM locations. Each year, volunteers at our warehouses, field bases, DRS projects, and other locations donate over 200,000 hours of work.

CAM's ultimate purpose is to glorify God and help enlarge His kingdom. ". . . whatsoever ye do, do all to the glory of God" (1 Cor. 10:31).

The Way to God & Peace

WE LIVE IN A WORLD OF SIN. SIN IS ANYTHING that goes against God's holy standards. When people do not follow the guidelines that God their Creator gave them, they are guilty of sin. Choosing to sin separates us from God, the source of life.

Unfortunately, sin is universal. The Bible says that we all have "sinned and come short of the glory of God" (Romans 3:23). It also says that the natural consequence for that sin is eternal death, or punishment in an eternal hell: "Then when lust hath conceived, it bringeth forth sin: and sin, when it is finished, bringeth forth death" (James 1:15).

But eternal death is not inevitable. We do not have to be condemned to hell. God provided forgiveness for our sins through the death of His only Son, Jesus Christ. Because Jesus was perfect and without sin, he could die in our place. Because Jesus endured death, we do not have to die eternally.

A sacrifice is something given to benefit someone else. It is something that costs the giver greatly. Jesus was God's sacrifice that He gave to benefit us. Jesus' death takes away the penalty of sin for everyone who receives this gift and accepts the fact that through it he can be saved from eternal death. "For God so loved the world that he gave his only begotten Son, that whosoever believeth in him should not perish, but have everlasting life" (John 3:16).

In order to experience reconciliation with God, and eternal life in heaven rather than eternal death in hell, we must also repent of our sins (Deuteronomy 30:19). To repent of sins means to be truly sorry for the things we have done that have violated God's standards. It also means turning away from these sins (Acts 2:38; 3:19; 17:30).

By receiving the gift of Jesus as our sacrifice and repenting of our sins, we become new creatures with new desires and attitudes (2 Corinthians 5:17). In the same way that Jesus conquered death and is alive today, we can also conquer our sinful, selfish desires and experience a brand new life (Romans 6:4). This means that we do not continue in sin, but will yield to the new desires in our hearts and make choices that please God (1 John 3:9). We will testify to others of this new life by being baptized and sharing about what God has done for us.

Once we have become new creatures, we want to continue growing spiritually. We will be happy to let Jesus be the Master of our lives and will want to become more like Him, our perfect example. In order to do this, we must meditate on God's Word and commune with God in prayer. Fellowship with a faithful group of believers will also strengthen and maintain our walk with God (1 John 1:7). If we do fail and commit sins, we can come to God and ask forgiveness. "If we confess our sins, he is faithful and just to forgive us our sins, and to cleanse us from all unrighteousness" (1 John 1:9).